MW01075691

# How to Write a Resume: The Complete Guide to Modern Resume Writing

By Inklyo.com

Print Edition

ISBN: 978-0-9950480-5-8
ISBN-13: 978-1535270823

For permission requests, please contact us online or write to:

Inklyo Inc.

405 Riverview Drive, Suite 304

Chatham, Ontario N7M 0N3

Attention: E-Book Inquiry

www.inklyo.com

Printed in Canada

ISBN: 978-0-9950480-5-8

# CONTENTS

# 1 TELLING THE STORY OF YOU: WHY RESUMES ARE MORE IMPORTANT THAN YOU THINK

Resume writing is certainly not the most thrilling subject you will ever study, but it is important. As grumpy as properly formatting our objectives and employment histories may make us, no one can dispute the importance and usefulness of a well-crafted resume.

*Obviously*, you're probably thinking to yourself, *but what* is *a well-crafted resume*? That, my friends, is the question. (Don't tell Prince Hamlet.) Take a look at the following four examples of different people looking for jobs:

> An eager recent graduate is ready to put her academic and volunteer experience to good use and is looking to gain some much-needed work experience.

> A stay-at-home dad gets a call from his wife, who tells him she landed that big job she applied for on the other side of the country. Their children are nearly grown, so he decides that he, too, should start searching for an exciting new opportunity.

> An elementary-school teacher has had enough of second graders. After two decades in the teaching profession, he decides an office job is just what he needs. He starts looking into educational publishing.

A large factory closes after 30 years of business. Nearly 200 employees lose their jobs, and many of them lose their pensions as well. What do they do now?

These examples all represent individuals with different job-seeking needs. How can the graduate find a job when she has no work experience to showcase on her resume? How will the stay-at-home dad re-enter the job market after a 10-year absence? What kind of resume will help the elementary-school teacher make a major career change (and seriously reduce his stress levels)? And finally, how can the factory employees find good jobs that will allow them to support their families?

As you can see, knowing how to write a good resume can be *very* important.

But why am I telling you this? You're reading this book—you clearly understand the importance of having a well-crafted resume. I'm sure you also know that your job search will depend on many factors, like location, changes in the economy, your own qualifications, and employer expectations. You already know that finding a job can be tough; it's something you've heard before, time and time again. But what you don't know, and what you *haven't* heard, is which specific tools can help you get the job you want and deserve.

You may have sought the answer to this question and found many conflicting answers. One source says objective statements are outdated, while the next says these statements are absolutely necessary. Some experts assert that references should be provided upon request only, while others insist that references should always be included. Some people even argue that resumes are becoming obsolete entirely, saying that employers now prefer tools like LinkedIn and TalentBin to evaluate a candidate's qualifications. You, like most normal people, probably don't really care about any of this inconsistency. You just want a job, and you don't have time to sort the good information from the bad advice. Here's the good news: this frustration has brought you here, to this ebook—a simple and comprehensive guide to resume writing.

While we can't predict the future, we can prepare for it. While some people may think resumes are on their way out, the truth is that job seekers still need a method of letting employers know why they are ideal candidates, and employers still need a way to assess potential employees. That need is something that hasn't changed in decades. However, the requirements for creating a stellar resume are always evolving. Generic, one-size-fits-all documents just don't work anymore. Not only does your resume need to be uniquely designed for *your* information, it must also be tuned to the job you are applying for. On top of that demanding requirement, your resume must be tailored to accommodate applicant tracking systems that scan for specific keywords. Yes, there certainly is a lot to learn . . . and *How to Write a Resume: The Complete Guide to Modern Resume Writing* is here to teach you.

This ebook is full of proven tips and tricks for packing your resume-writing repertoire with the techniques you need to stand out to employers. This guide will lead you through the process of creating a resume from scratch, selecting a resume format that is best suited to your background, and understanding what information to include. With tons of examples and even a few sample resumes to choose from, this guide will teach you the principles you need to know and how to apply them to your own resume. So what are we waiting for? Let's get started! Say What You Mean and Mean What You Say: How to Craft the Language of Your Resume

### *Say What You Mean and Mean What You Say: How to Craft the Language of Your Resume*

### Introduction

Adopted from the French term *résumé*, meaning a summary or synopsis, a resume is a document meant to highlight your skills and showcase your potential in a few well-constructed pages. This can be tough. You, of course, are intimately familiar with your own education, employment, and volunteer work history. After all, you lived these experiences, and they helped shape the person you are today.

You know the primary duties and responsibilities that were required of you in each role, and you also know what skills you acquired from these experiences. The trick now is to translate your knowledge about your own history into clear, professional language that highlights and markets your skills to potential employers. Sounds easy, right? Just write everything down and wait for the job offers to fly in. Piece of cake.

But what if I told you that the language you use to describe your skills is every bit as important as your career history and experience? Or that every word in your resume should be carefully selected to work in your favor? You would probably make a point of learning the conventions of resume lingo and form, right?

There are eight main things to keep in mind when it comes to the language you use in your resume. We'll cover them all in a bit more detail throughout this chapter:

- ✓ Use a variety of strong action verbs to highlight your accomplishments, and avoid personal pronouns to keep the focus where it needs to be

- ✓ Remove small words like articles (*a, an, the*), helping verbs (e.g., *have, had, might*), and personal pronouns (e.g., *I, my*), and try to be brief

- ✓ Use correct (and consistent) tenses

- ✓ Avoid generic language by using quantitative descriptions of your duties and accomplishments, and avoid wordiness

- ✓ Avoid the use of "buzzwords;" use solid examples instead

- ✓ Avoid using jargon or undefined acronyms

✓ Use keywords from the job posting to accommodate applicant tracking systems (ATSs)

✓ Make sure your resume is free of all errors

If this list overwhelms you, or if you're questioning *how* to do some of these things, fear not; we're going to break down each of these points and explain them.

## Using Action Verbs and Avoiding Personal Pronouns

A solid understanding of English grammar conventions is a great skill to have when writing a resume. You certainly don't want to use a document riddled with errors when you're trying to demonstrate your competence.

But being a grammar expert does not necessarily make you a resume expert, as the conventions of resume lingo sometimes differ from English grammar rules. You'll see some of these differences as we discuss how action verbs and personal pronouns are used (and not used) in resumes.

### *Action verbs*

When it comes to highlighting your job accomplishments, you want the focus to be on the accomplishments themselves, not on how you performed them. This is why you should use strong, direct action statements to highlight your accomplishments throughout your career. For example:

>**Don't** say this:

>I worked as the manager of a small sales team.

>**Do** say this:

>Managed a sales team of 12 employees.

In the first sentence, the focus is on the person who wrote the resume.

In the second, the emphasis is on the action the person performed (*managed*). The great thing about action verbs is that there are tons of them. There is really no need to repeat verbs within your resume. Just look at all these action verbs:

- Monitored
- Instructed
- Managed
- Influenced
- Guided
- Evaluated
- Modified
- Revised
- Developed
- Approved
- Built
- Planned
- Refined
- Streamlined
- Analyzed
- Documented
- Reviewed
- Restructured
- Organized
- Examined
- Regulated
- Prepared
- Arranged
- Ordered
- Coordinated

There are so many action verbs to choose from, one hardly knows where to begin! Whenever possible, use action verbs instead of generic "skill" words like *creativity*, *leadership*, or *communication*. Instead of stating that you are capable of these sometimes abstract concepts, show *how* you demonstrate these concepts using concrete examples with action verbs. Here are some verbs that can be used in place of generic skills, along with some examples of how the verbs can be used to illustrate actual accomplishments.

Instead of *creativity*, try one of these action verbs: brainstormed, constructed, designed.

Regularly **brainstormed** ideas for future marketing plans during meetings with team

**Constructed** timetable with key dates for completion of important tasks

**Designed** software programs to fit company's unique accounting needs

Instead of *leadership*, try one of these action verbs: established, expanded, improved.

**Established** training protocol for new employees

**Expanded** on existing training material by creating companion video

**Improved** efficiency of HR processes by reducing the number of steps required to hire new employees

Instead of *communication*, try one of these action verbs: persuaded, clarified, corresponded.

**Persuaded** upper management to increase transparency of basic business processes

**Clarified** complex instructions and unique job responsibilities for junior employees

**Corresponded** with future conference participants, answering questions and resolving    sign-up difficulties

Next is an example of the employment section of a resume created in response to a specific job post. Notice how action verbs are used to demonstrate the applicant's qualifications.

---

**Software Developer**

We are currently seeking a full-time software developer for our office in Chatham, Ontario. As a software developer, you will develop new proprietary software and site code for Scribendi Inc. and its associated web properties using the best software development practices; provide incremental improvements to existing software and website code; and provide analysis and debugging of existing and new code as required.

**Nature of Work:**

Programming and web development primarily using, but not restricted to, PHP, MySQL, JavaScript, jQuery, AJAX, HTML5, CSS3, and APIs.

**Specific Skills:**

- A solid understanding of web applications work, including security, session management, and best development practices.
- Adequate knowledge of relational database systems, object-oriented programming, and web application development.
- Strong grasp of web application security principals.
- Strong code organization with proper indentation, commenting, and documentation.
- Deep functional knowledge or hands on design experience with web services (REST, SOAP, etc.).
- Ability to work and thrive in a fast-paced environment and learn rapidly and master diverse web technologies and techniques.
- Strong communication, organizational, and time management skills.
- Proven problem-solving and analytical skills.
- The ability to learn quickly and continuously.
- The ability to work both independently and with others.

---

PROFESSIONAL EXPERIENCE
**Software Developer**
*Ticketmaster, Toronto, Ontario, Canada*                    2010–Present
- Write and edit software code
- Ensure that web security protocol is followed
- Adhere to best practices in development, design, and security

**Programmer**                                              2008–2010
*Scotia Bank, Toronto, Ontario, Canada*
- Maintained relational databases
- Designed algorithms using JavaScript, Python, HTML5, MySQL, and CSS3
- Modified computer programs as required

**Help Desk Technician**                                    2003–2007
*University of Toronto Libraries, Toronto, Ontario, Canada*
- Assisted students, faculty, and staff with their use of computers, printers, and photocopy machines
- Monitored the network, resolving problems as they arose
- Developed instructional documents and materials to advise users of proper use of computers, printers, etc.

For this job posting, the applicant should consider using a skills section to ensure that the resume addresses all the required skills outlined in the job post. For more information on the skills section of a resume, see "Which Type of Resume Are You?" and "Time to Start Writing: Everything You Need to Know about the 8 Resume Sections."

Whatever the skill or accomplishment, there is surely a perfect action verb to describe it. One other thing to remember: the goal is to demonstrate your skills, abilities, and accomplishments, not to misrepresent or exaggerate the extent of your experience. Fudging your resume details may seem like a really great idea until you find yourself unable to answer questions in an interview that you're not qualified to be in. The "fake it till you make it" approach may have somehow gotten you through your beginner university courses, but it will not serve you well in your hunt for the perfect job.

## Personal pronouns

Just like using action verbs is a great way to keep the focus on your actions, so too is avoiding the use of personal pronouns (e.g., *my* or *I*) to describe your job duties and professional accomplishments. Remember, when it comes to resume writing, your actual actions are the star of the show. Here are a couple of examples.

**Don't** say this:

*I* helped develop a project management system to improve the company's internal communication.

**Do** say this:

Developed a project management system to improve the company's internal communication.

Got it? Here's one more example.

**Don't** say this:

*I* coordinated workshop registration, and *I* also helped prepare workshop handouts for participants.

**Do** say this:

Coordinated workshop registration and prepared workshop handouts for participants.

The employment section of the following resume does not use personal pronouns.

PROFESSIONAL EXPERIENCE
**Health Information Specialist**
*Toronto General Hospital, Toronto, Ontario, Canada*                    2003–Present
- Respond to information queries from patients, staff, and visitors
- Develop and maintain physical and digital collections of current, high-quality information resources
- Deliver presentations to health professionals and other staff on the use of health information databases

**Teaching Assistant**
*University of Western Ontario, London, Ontario, Canada*                    2000–2002
- Replied to student emails promptly and efficiently
- Graded student assignments
- Held office hours to assist students with course concepts and other related issues

**Part-Time Sales Associate**
*Sears, London, Ontario, Canada*                    1999–2002
- Interacted with customers in an engaging, friendly manner
- Used active listening techniques to fully comprehend customer needs
- Ensured that the store consistently remained clean, orderly, and organized

## Removing Articles and Helping Verbs

Articles (*a*, *an*, *the*) and helping verbs (e.g., *have*, *had*, *might*) can sometimes be eliminated to improve the strength with which your message is delivered. This is especially true for descriptions of job duties. Sometimes, an article is essential to retaining the meaning of the sentence. If you're not sure, it's probably safer to keep an article in than to remove it. In most resumes, however, the number of articles and helping verbs can be seriously reduced. Take a look at these examples:

> **Don't** say this:
>
> > I streamlined **the** office processes.
>
> **Do** say this:
>
> > Streamlined office processes.

In the above example, the personal pronoun *I* and the article *the* have both been removed, but the meaning of the sentence has been retained. Let's look at one more.

> **Don't** say this:
>
> > I **was** responsible for responding to student queries through email in **a** professional and timely manner.
>
> **Do** say this:
>
> > Responded to student email queries professionally and
> quickly.

You'll notice that in the above example, it was not possible to simply remove the helping verb (*was*) and article (*a*). The sentence had to be slightly restructured. In restructuring this sentence, we were also able to make it concise in other ways. The practices demonstrated above not only make language more direct, they also save space on your resume. Keeping your language short and to the point is also incredibly helpful for your potential employer, who will certainly already have pages and pages of resumes to read through. Brevity is a job-seeker's best friend. (Sorry, Fido.)

The example below is an employment section of a resume that does not use articles or helping verbs. Notice that the essential meaning of the information is maintained.

---

**EMPLOYMENT**

**Medical Receptionist**
*Cornerstone Physiotherapy, Toronto, Ontario, Canada*      2010–Present
- Schedule appointments and organize patient referrals
- Respond to patient inquiries via phone
- Update patient files and information

**Office Assistant**
*The City of Windsor, Windsor, Ontario, Canada*      2007–2010
- Greeted all visitors
- Answered phone calls, emails, and faxes
- Ensured that office equipment remained in proper working order

**Sales Advisor**
*Ardene, Windsor, Ontario, Canada*      2005–2007
- Kept customers informed of sales and promotions
- Stocked and displayed store merchandise
- Attended to customer needs promptly and efficiently

---

## Using Correct and Consistent Tense

Another simple (though important) rule regarding resume lingo is to be consistent in your use of tense. Use the present tense to describe your current position. Use the past tense to describe previous jobs. Do not shift tenses when describing your duties at a single position.

Here is an example of a job description written using *inconsistent* tense.

> *Student Intern*
> Center for English Language Education, Windsor, Ontario, 2010–2012
> - **Instructed** a group of high school students on the elements of proper English grammar, spelling, and punctuation
> - **Design** learning objectives with which the students are evaluated

In this example, the past tense (*instructed*) is used for one point, while the present tense (*design*) is used for the next. Since this individual is no longer employed as a student intern, *instructed* and *design* should both be written in the past tense (*instructed* and *designed*).

Here is an example in which the tense is consistent.

> *Customer Service Representative*
> Goodlife Fitness, London, Ontario, 2007–2010
> - **Greeted** incoming members in a friendly, courteous manner
> - **Answered** questions and addressed concerns from members
> - **Renewed** memberships as necessary

## Avoiding Generic Language and Writing with Concision

Avoid generic language whenever possible. You should also steer clear of excessively complex phrasing or descriptions. Most employers have a knack for identifying applicants who have embellished to fill space or make their career seem more impressive.

For example:

> "Facilitated the management of" can be simplified as "managed," and

> "Engaged in the development of" can be simplified as "developed."

While using keywords from the job description is smart, do not simply regurgitate this information. Give the employer the specifics about your unique career path. We'll get into more detail about using keywords later in the chapter.

Let's look at a more in-depth example. Let's say you're applying for a job that requires applicants to have extensive experience in administrative office work.

    **Don't** say this:

        Extensive experience in administrative office work.

Not only is the above sentence generic, but it also tells the employer absolutely nothing about your actual skills or experience. Let's try it again using greater detail, but with the same concise language that has been discussed throughout the chapter.

    **Do** say this:

        Experience in administrative office work, including filing records and reports, scheduling appointments, and maintaining office equipment.

Here is an example of a resume that is unnecessarily wordy, with the excessively wordy language underlined.

---

EMPLOYMENT EXPERIENCE
**Instruction and Information Literacy Librarian**
*University of Toronto Libraries, Toronto, Ontario, Canada*     2008–Present
- Engage in the development of information literacy tutorials for undergraduate students, graduate students, and faculty
- Involved with the design of information literacy tutorials for various user groups
- Responsible for the creation of workshop materials and handouts, as well as learning objectives

**Library Technician**
*London Public Library, London, Ontario, Canada*     2004–2008
- Assisted with providing reference help to all library users
- Helped with circulating and shelving library materials
- Responsible for performing clerical functions as needed

---

Now, let's revise this by removing unnecessary words and simplifying the language.

---

**EMPLOYMENT EXPERIENCE**
**Instruction and Information Literacy Librarian**
*University of Toronto Libraries, Toronto, Ontario, Canada*          2008–Present
  - Develop information literacy tutorials for undergraduate students, graduate students, and faculty
  - Design information literacy tutorials for various user groups
  - Create workshop materials and handouts, as well as learning objectives

**Library Technician**
*London Public Library, London, Ontario, Canada*          2004–2008
  - Provided reference assistance to all library users
  - Circulated and shelved library materials
  - Performed clerical functions as needed

---

You can also avoid being generic by quantifying your experiences whenever possible. Quantifying your experiences shows your potential employer *exactly* what you have accomplished in previous roles, which gives them a great idea of what you're capable of. Let's look at one example of using quantification to *show* an accomplishment rather than using description to *tell* about it.

For example:

Instead of noting that you consistently improved your company's sale margin, say:

Exceeded sales targets by 20% over a 2-month period.

## Avoiding Buzzwords

Certain buzzwords used in resumes are almost guaranteed to elicit an eye roll from an employer. Think overused descriptors like *hardworking*, *team player*, and *detail oriented.* These "soft skills" are often included in job descriptions, but this does not mean that you should merely state that you have them. Instead, demonstrate that you have these skills using specific examples. Here are some overused buzzwords to avoid using in your resume:

- Results oriented
- Proactive
- Eager to learn

- Self-motivated
- Excellent communication skills

- Track record of proven success • Good interpersonal skills

- Strong organizational skills • Excellent time-management skills

Don't bother telling your prospective employer that you're hardworking and a team player. Instead, describe the accomplishments you have achieved as a result of your dedication and ability to work with others. Provide concrete details and relevant examples of success.

Though we've already looked at many examples of *showing* rather than *telling*, one more can't hurt. Take a look at this example of how buzzwords like those listed above can be avoided.

> **Don't** say this:

> Proven track record of success.

> **Do** say this:

> Increased department revenue by 13.7% in 2013 fiscal year after implementation of new sales tracking system.

## Avoiding Jargon and Undefined Acronyms

Avoid using unclear acronyms or industry-specific jargon—unless these terms are appropriate for the position to which you are applying and you are sure that the individual in charge of hiring will understand them. While industry-specific terminology is potentially beneficial in a resume that will be submitted to an employer who is accustomed to these terms, such terminology may confuse employers or hiring managers who are unfamiliar with the field.

Even for employers who are familiar with industry jargon, a resume loaded with acronyms is difficult to read. Take this sentence, for example, which uses many commonly known abbreviations. (Please note that this sentence has most definitely not been taken from a resume and is being used only for the sake of example.)

OMG, my BF said ILY yesterday.

You likely know that those initialisms stand for *oh my god*, *boyfriend*, and *I love you*, but that knowledge certainly didn't make reading that sentence any less annoying, did it?

## Using Keywords to Accommodate Applicant Tracking Systems (ATSs)

The online recruitment process has become more sophisticated, and many applicants have no idea that these developments can influence their job prospects. The traditional hiring process of reading through paper resumes to find an ideal candidate has been replaced not only by online application forms but also by applicant tracking systems (ATSs).

An ATS is software that automatically scans hundreds of applications for information related to job postings, including keywords, employment history, past employers, and educational background. The ATS then uses the information to determine if an applicant will move forward in the hiring process. Typically, applicants upload their resumes to an online job system that has been programmed according to an employer's specific requirements.

Though these systems are generally quite accurate in their ability to narrow the field of potential candidates, the effectiveness of these systems can vary among companies, making it very easy for resumes to become overlooked. So, what can you do to ensure your resume is seen? You can include keywords directly from the job description.

Keywords

- are terms or phrases representing required qualifications

- may be names of degrees, company names, dates of employment, school names, etc.

- may be unique industry terms

- can represent the primary responsibilities for a position

Here is an example job description of an opening for a sales manager. This description is embedded with keywords (underlined in this example) that the hiring manager has likely programmed the ATS to identify.

**Job Title**: Sales manager
**Job Type**: Full time
**Education**: Some university and/or equivalent combination of education and experience
**Salary**: Commensurate with experience
**Job Duties**:

- Design monthly sales and marketing plans
- Supervise other staff members and ensure that monthly sales quotas are met
- Follow policy guidelines for corrective measures when performance goals are not met
- Regularly liaise with the heads of other departments within the organization
- Train new staff members and sales associates
- Attend monthly training sessions with staff members to ensure that product knowledge remains current

**Required Experience**:

- Five to seven years of sales experience, preferably in a retail environment
- Demonstrated experience with customer service
- Demonstrated ability to work in a fast-paced environment in both an individual and a team capacity
- Proven track record of meeting (and exceeding) sales quotas
- Proficiency with computer applications, namely Outlook, Word, and Excel
- Strong verbal and written communication skills
- Experience in a managerial role is an asset

When scanning resumes, ATSs will evaluate resumes based on keyword density to determine which candidates will move forward in the hiring process. This is why it is so important to make sure you have included these keywords in your resume. Bear in mind that ATSs are *very* black and white in the way they filter resumes according to keywords—if the necessary keywords are not present, then the ATS will automatically skip over the resume.

How do you know which keywords you should be using? Pay attention to repeated words or phrases in a job posting; these are usually the most important elements of the job. The name of the position itself (e.g., sales manager) is also a useful clue when searching for keywords.

In the example job descriptions below, the main keywords are underlined.

- Must have extensive experience with writing learning objectives

- Must have knowledge of and experience with implementing active learning techniques

- Must have extensive knowledge of the current English curriculum

- A degree in English literature and a Bachelor of Education (B.Ed) are required

Try to embed these keywords in your career or professional summary at the beginning of your resume, as well as in the descriptions beneath each job title. Be sure to edit and proofread your resume carefully, because ATSs won't register your keywords if they are misspelled!

### Customizing Your Resume

If there's one thing we hope you've taken from this book so far, it's this: the more you put into writing your resume, the more you will get out of it. Key to this point is customizing your resume for each position. Though it may be much easier to send a generic resume to several potential employers, this method is not likely to get you a strong response. If your resume does not provide your potential employer with *a clear link between the job description and your resume*, then the employer will pass over your resume without hesitation.

Here are the main elements to keep in mind when tailoring your resume for a specific position:

☆ Consider the job title, primary duties/responsibilities associated with the position, specific educational requirements, and keywords used within the job description.

☆ Customize your formatting depending on the type of job you are applying for. If you are using a resume template as a guideline, be sure to customize your resume.

☆ Adjust the length of your resume to fit the position to which you are applying. Generally, a resume should be kept at two pages in length. However, for positions requiring that candidates have 10+ years of work experience in a specific field, a longer resume (and possibly a CV) may be more appropriate.

☆ Write your resume according to the customs of the country or region in which you are applying for a job.

## Customizing based on job description

The following resume elements should be customized based on the details of the job to which you are applying:

• Objective statement

• Job descriptions

• Skills profile

Perhaps the best way to determine how to customize these elements is to look at an example.

Let's look at a customized resume for a specific position. The candidate's name is Julie, and she's looking to apply for a position as a legal assistant in a law office. Here is the job description for the position:

**Job Title**: Legal assistant

**Job Type**: Full time

**Education**: A university degree in a related field or a relevant combination of experience and education

**Salary**: Negotiable

**Job Duties**:

- Assist lawyers in the firm with conducting legal research for cases and preparing court documents
- Draft legal correspondences, memos, and letters
- Assist lawyers with preparation for trial and pre-trial
- Organize client documents and files in an electronic system

**Required Experience:**

- Excellent computer skills
- Excellent verbal and written communication skills
- Typing speed of at least 60 words per minute
- Demonstrated organizational skills
- Ability to work independently and as part of a team
- Some knowledge of the legal system will be considered an asset

Julie has never worked in a law office before, but she has significant past experience with office work and has completed several courses in law. Julie must make sure that the job descriptions for her past administrative positions highlight her computer skills, typing speed, communication skills, and ability to disseminate information to fellow employees and clients.

Julie must also make sure that she mentions the specific law courses that she has taken. She should also consider rearranging the elements of her resume (employment history, education, volunteer experience, certificates, etc.) to highlight the most relevant components of her qualifications, as appropriate. Because Julie has completed specific courses that are relevant to the legal assistant position, she should place her education history before her employment history.

Here is Julie's original resume, before she tailored it to the specific job post:

---

# Julie Smith

355 Dundas St • London, Ontario, Canada • N7L 5Y6
**CELL** (231) 645-7890 • **EMAIL** j.a.smith@email.com

| | |
|---|---|
| PROFILE | Experienced professional with over five years of experience in office work and administration. |

| | | |
|---|---|---|
| EMPLOYMENT | **Receptionist/Administrative Assistant** | |
| | BMO Financial Group, London, Ontario | 2005–Present |
| | • Maintained files and assisted with document preparation | |
| | • Managed client accounts | |
| | • Complied with administrative policies | |
| | **Student Office Assistant** | 2002–2004 |
| | Registrar's Office, University of Windsor, London, Ontario | |
| | • Provided administrative support to the office manager | |
| | • Replied to in-person, phone, and email inquiries from students | |
| | • Assisted students with questions regarding registration and completing registration forms | |

| | | |
|---|---|---|
| VOLUNTEERING | **Records Management** | |
| | City Centre Archives, London, Ontario | 2002–2005 |
| | • Ensured that files were safe and undamaged | |
| | • Updated records as required | |
| | • Transferred paper records to electronic format | |

| | | |
|---|---|---|
| EDUCATION | **Bachelor of Art in History** | |
| | University of Western Ontario, London, Ontario | 2000–2004 |
| | Graduated with 4.0 GPA | |

---

In the example above, Julie has failed to note that she has taken law courses as part of her education. She also does not mention her typing speed or computer skills. Therefore, the individual reviewing her resume may fail to see a link between Julie's qualifications and the requirements of the positon.

Here is Julie's revised resume, which has been tailored to fit the job description:

# Julie Smith

355 Dundas St • London, Ontario, Canada • N7L 5Y6
**CELL** (231) 645-7890 • **EMAIL** j.a.smith@email.com

| | |
|---|---|
| PROFILE | Experienced professional with over five years of progressive experience in office work and administration. Typing speed of 70 words per minute. Proficient in using Microsoft Office Suite (Word, Excel, PowerPoint) and organizing files in file management systems. |

EDUCATION

**Bachelor of Art in History**
University of Western Ontario, London, Ontario                2000–2004
- Graduated with 4.0 GPA
- Successfully completed multiple law courses: Legal Research and Writing, Criminal Law, and Torts

EMPLOYMENT

**Receptionist/Administrative Assistant**
BMO Financial Group, London, Ontario                2005–Present
- Maintained files and assisted with document preparation
- Managed client accounts
- Complied with administrative policies

**Student Office Assistant**                2002–2004
Registrar's Office, University of Windsor, London, Ontario
- Provided administrative support to the office manager
- Replied to in-person, phone, and email inquiries from students
- Assisted students with questions regarding registration and completing registration forms

VOLUNTEERING **Records Management**
City Centre Archives, London, Ontario                2002–2005
- Ensured that files were safe and undamaged
- Updated records as required
- Transferred paper records to electronic format

## Ensuring Your Resume is Free of Errors

Are you really detail oriented? Your first step to prove this to an employer is to create a well-written, grammatically correct resume. A simple review of many online resume "how-to" articles will tell you that using poor spelling and grammar is a fantastic way to eliminate your chances as a potential job candidate. Obviously, failure to pay attention to details on something as important as a resume demonstrates an inability to focus on small, crucial details, but more than that, it demonstrates carelessness. If you can't be bothered to proofread your own resume, how can the employer count on you to do other things, like show up for work on time? Or meet deadlines? Or, you know, proofread the work you do for them?

If you don't feel secure enough in your own grammatical skills, have a friend review your resume. If you don't have a grammatically inclined friend, consider checking out a professional editing and proofreading service (such as Scribendi, which offers affordable and quality editing services). Seriously. It's that important.

There you have it—the principles of resume language. Pretty straightforward, right? Okay, so maybe it's a lot to digest. But now that you know *how* to write your resume, it's time to address the next challenge: deciding which resume format is right for you.

# 2 WHICH RESUME TYPE ARE YOU? ALL ABOUT CHRONOLOGICAL, FUNCTIONAL, AND COMBINATION RESUMES

You may resent the implication that you can be sorted so easily into a "type," but when it comes to your job search, using a certain resume type can actually be a great way to show exactly why you, with your specific employment history and experience, are the best candidate for the job. Selecting the appropriate resume format is a good way to emphasize your strengths and minimize any potential weaknesses you may have (for example, gaps in your employment history).

In this chapter, we will discuss three tried-and-true resume formats and the basic sections that should be included in each type. We'll help you decide which format is best suited to you and your experience.

The three basic resume types are

- ✓ Chronological — Useful if you have a stable work history, have progressively achieved positions with greater responsibility, and have significant experience in your field; or if your professional experience relates closely to the position to which you are applying.

✓ Functional — Useful if you have a diverse work history, are hoping to enter a new field, are re-entering the workforce, or if you have gaps in your employment history.

✓ Combination — Useful if you have a steady employment history but are still making advancements in your chosen field, or if you have specific skills you would like to highlight.

## The Chronological Resume

_What to include in a chronological resume_

This format is what you most likely think of when you hear the word _resume_. Generally, a chronological resume includes the following sections:

☆ Contact information

☆ A career summary, executive profile, or objective statement

☆ A chronological employment history, with the most current position listed first

☆ A chronological listing of your volunteer history, if applicable

☆ Education

You may choose to include other sections (such as awards and achievements or references sections), depending on your specific experience and the requirements of the specific position (find more information on the common sections of a resume in "Time to Start Writing: Everything You Need to Know about the 8 Resume Sections").

As the name suggests, the chronological resume presents your career history in a reverse chronology (with your most recent employment first). Everything we covered about employment history in the previous chapter applies here. Just to recap: the employment section can be named "Experience," "Employment History," or "Professional

Experience," and it provides the details (including primary job duties and achievements) pertaining to each position. The chronological resume also includes other details, including professional affiliations and educational history.

### When to use a chronological resume

Chronological resumes may be the most popular format, but that doesn't mean this type of resume is best for you. A chronological resume will work best for you if:

- You have had positions with progressively more responsibility

- You have had a stable, uninterrupted employment history

- You are a student or a recent graduate with experience in your chosen field

- Your professional experience closely relates to the position to which you are applying

The great thing about this resume format is that it allows employers to easily see when you were employed with previous companies and what your primary job responsibilities were. The sad truth is that your prospective employer probably won't want to spend a ton of time looking at your resume. A chronological resume is easy to scan, thereby allowing the employer to quickly evaluate your skills and experience.

### When not to use a chronological resume

The main downfall of the chronological resume format is that it really highlights any potential flaws or gaps in your employment. If you have something you'd rather not bring attention to, you should avoid the chronological format. Here are some specific circumstances in which a chronological resume is not the best choice:

- You have large gaps in employment

- You have limited professional experience in your field or are trying to transition to another field

- You have changed positions frequently in the past

*Chronological resume sample*

Here is a sample of a chronological resume:

---

# JAMES MORIARTY

187 North Gower St · Camden London, UK · (555) 359-6666 · criminalmastermind@getsherlock.com

OBJECTIVE
To undermine the efforts of and eventually remove from this earth one Sherlock Holmes, Private Detective. While my earlier aspirations focused on building London's ring of criminal activity to the national and then international level, in recent years I have realized that to accomplish this goal, I must first solve the final problem that is Mr. Sherlock Holmes. Willing to take out Dr. John Watson, if necessary, though I would prefer to use him as leverage against his dear friend Mr. Holmes.

ACHIEVEMENTS
| | |
|---|---|
| Won the American Mafia's Consultant of the Year Award | 1885 |
| Named Mr. Congeniality by the British Mafia | 1886 |
| Caused the fake death and subsequent two-year hiatus of Sherlock Holmes | 1891 |

EDUCATION
**Master of Mathematics**                                    April 1881
*University of Cambridge*, Cambridge, UK
Completed thesis: *Dynamics of an Asteroid*

**Bachelor of Science in Mathematics**                       April 1877
*University of Oxford*, Oxford, UK

EMPLOYMENT
**Consulting Criminal**
*Moriarty's Criminal Consulting*, London, UK                 June 1888–Present
- Began the world's first Consulting Criminal business, which is based on the important notion that every fairy tale needs a good old-fashioned villain
- Built own criminal network based on connections made in previous positions with different criminal organizations; made use of an extensive marketing strategy to grow business
- Stole the Crown Jewels, broke into the Bank of England, and facilitated a riot at Pentonville Prison, all in one morning
- Destroyed Sherlock Holmes' credibility and favor with the public through an intricately planned and executed scheme

**Managing Consultant**                                      May 1886–June 1888
*British Mafia*, London, UK
- Organized the assassination of several prominent London figures while never engaging in activity that would lead to conviction on any related charges
- Increased capital by 88% in just two years

**Consultant**                                               October 1884–May 1886
*American Mafia*, New York, USA

---

34

- Worked under the instruction of more senior mobsters to organize small but essential operations in New York as well as in other Mafia jurisdictions internationally
- Learned the ins and outs of managing the budget for a large crime organization

**Freelance Bank Robber**                                      April 1881–October 1884
London, UK
- Organized bank robberies to meet the needs of specific clients
- Kept all involved parties out of prison, except for those who failed to follow clear instructions
- My work as a freelancer caught the attention of American Mafia bosses, who then recruited me for work in New York City

VOLUNTEERING
**Chair**                                                          July 1885–Present
*Little Criminals Organization (LCO)*, London, UK
- Organize events to encourage children to pursue careers in the criminal arts
- Run workshops to teach basic crime skills, including lock picking, computer hacking, and psychological manipulation

**Dog Walker**                                                   January 1877–Present
*Royal Society for the Prevention of Cruelty to Animals*, London, UK

## The Functional Resume

*What to include in a functional resume*

The functional resume lists job-specific skills in clearly defined categories. This format presents your core competencies and responsibilities and can include other categories that demonstrate your suitability for a job (administrative skills, computer skills, customer service experience, etc.). Within each of these categories, examples of your achievements are provided that demonstrate your experience in these areas.

Because a functional resume format really focuses on your specific competencies, the sections included are a bit more fluid. These are the sections most commonly seen in functional resumes:

- ☆ Contact Information

- ☆ An objective statement, professional profile, or executive summary

- ☆ A skills summary

- ☆ A detailed section (sometimes titled "Experience" or

"Professional Experience") that includes various subcategories of skills relevant to the position

☆ Employment history

☆ Education

This format removes the focus from job titles, places of employment, or dates of employment. Instead, it highlights the professional skills that you believe would benefit an employer the most. Because this format emphasizes the professional skills that you can bring to a job, the functional resume is a good option if your career path has been irregular or somewhat erratic. Dates and places of employment are occasionally (though not often) omitted entirely, and career history and education are most often provided briefly at the end of the resume.

This example shows the "Experience" section of a functional resume. Notice how it differs from that of a chronological resume.

---

**PROFESSIONAL EXPERIENCE**

*Medical Knowledge and Practical Skills*
- Managed the simultaneous care of multiple patients, including monitoring the conditions and recovery of patients with illness and those who had undergone surgery
- Completed trauma training and practiced triaging in earlier positions as a nurse and a US Army medic
- Instructed support staff regarding patient care
- Maintained immaculate medical records, including patient charts during hospital stays and patient test results
- Specialized in trauma surgery, completing a residency at Stanford Health Care (SHC) in Stanford, California
- Administered anesthetics to patients undergoing dental procedures

*Teaching and Education Skills*
- Taught classes at different grade and age levels in multiple subjects, including math, science, computers, and geography
- Evaluated students' work and helped those who were struggling improve

*Organizational and Managerial Skills*
- Created surgery schedules and accommodated for emergency cases as they occurred
- Acted as a supervisor for less-experienced staff members
- Submitted evaluations to supervisors in a timely manner and completed all evaluations on schedule

---

### When to use a functional resume

The functional resume, though not as common as the chronological resume, can be very useful. The categories you include should give the employer confidence that you have the skills needed to excel at the job, regardless of whether you have had extensive experience within the field.

A functional resume will work best for you if:

- You have related, but not *directly* related, experience for the position to which you are applying

- You have a diverse work history

- You are hoping to enter a new field

- You are re-entering the workforce after a long period of unemployment

- You have jumped between jobs in the past or have some noticeable gaps in employment

- You have had many very similar jobs

- You are overqualified for a particular position

### When not to use a functional resume

The functional resume format can be very useful, but be wary of how you use this format. Some employers may see a functional resume and wonder what exactly the candidate is trying to hide. To avoid such suspicion, be sure to use headings that highlight occupational skills (sales experience, project management, customer service, administrative experience) rather than personal skills (problem solving, communication skills).

A functional resume may not be your best option if:

- You have held positions with progressively greater responsibility that you wish to highlight

- You have had a stable work history

*Functional resume example*

Here is an example of a functional resume:

## BARBARA MILLICENT ROBERTS

33 Continental Blvd • El Segundo, CA • 90245-5012
(+1) 310-252-3687 • workinggirl@therealbarbie.com

**EDUCATION**
PhD in Everything
University of Mattel
California, USA
March 1959
Graduated with honors

**SKILLS**
Basic Clinical Skills
Trauma Surgery
Triage
Dental Procedures and Surgery
Giving Lectures
Evaluating Student Work
Management and Leadership
Fashion

**EMPLOYMENT HISTORY**
Registered Nurse, 1961
Student Teacher, 1965
Surgeon, 1973
Veterinarian, 1985
Army Medic, 1993
Elementary Teacher, 1995
Dentist, 1997
Spanish Teacher, 2001
Art Teacher, 2002
Neonatal Physician, 2009

**OBJECTIVE** To gain employment with a respected university as a professor of medicine. My ultimate goal is to share my knowledge and experience with medical students aspiring to become skilled clinicians.

**PROFILE** An incredibly versatile professional with experience in almost every major field of work. In addition to my work as a respected public icon, I have a unique medical background that includes work in the veterinary and dental health fields. Having worked as a surgeon, neonatal specialist, nurse, and army medic, my background as a physician and medical caregiver speaks for itself.

In addition to this vast medical experience, I have experience working as a teacher at different levels of the education system. At this point in my career and life, it is my goal to inspire others to follow their own dreams and to be whatever they want to be.

**PROFESSIONAL EXPERIENCE**
*Medical Knowledge and Practical Skills*
- Managed the simultaneous care of multiple patients, including monitoring the conditions and recovery of patients with illnesses and those who had undergone surgery
- Completed trauma training and practiced triaging in earlier positions as a nurse and a US Army medic
- Instructed support staff regarding patient care
- Maintained immaculate medical records, including patient charts during hospital stays and patient test results
- Specialized in trauma surgery, completing a residency at Stanford Health Care (SHC) in Stanford, California
- Administered anesthetics to patients undergoing dental procedures

*Teaching and Education Skills*
- Taught classes at different grade and age levels in multiple subjects, including math, science, computers, and geography
- Evaluated students' work and helped those who were struggling improve

*Organizational and Managerial Skills*
- Created surgery schedules and accommodated for emergency cases as they occurred
- Acted as a supervisor for less-experienced staff members
- Submitted evaluations to supervisors in a timely manner and completed all evaluations on schedule

## The Combination Resume

A combination resume allows the job seeker to incorporate elements from both the chronological and functional resume formats. This type of resume includes skill-based categories (core competencies, career highlights, or professional skills) placed either above or below a chronological listing of your education and employment history.

A combination resume includes the following basic sections:

☆ Contact information

☆ An objective statement, career summary, or executive profile

☆ A profile of skills or skills summary

☆ A reverse chronology of your employment history

☆ Educational information

Including a chronological listing of your experience gives employers the *when* and *where* of your relevant employment history and shows the functional skills that you can offer to an employer. The format is flexible, allowing you to highlight your strongest assets, whether these include your education, professional skills, or work history. Finally, this format allows for more detailed information, which may improve retrieval via an ATS.

*When to use a combination resume*

You might consider using a combination resume if:

• You have a steady employment history but are still making advancements in your chosen field

• You have many specific skills or accomplishments to highlight in addition to your work history

### *When not to use a combination resume*

Though a combination resume is a great option for those with steady employment histories and specific skills they wish to highlight, there are several instances in which this resume format should be avoided:

- You have an extensive work history, and including a skills section would leave you with less room to outline the details of your career

- You have noticeable gaps in employment

- Some of your employment history is unrelated to the position to which you are applying (in this case, opt for a functional resume)

### *Combination resume example*

Here is an example of a combination resume:

# Michael Mouse

CONTACT

500 South Buena Vista St
Burbank, CA
91521-6369

CELL (818) 567-5151
mickeymouse@disney.com

www.disney.com

in   LINKEDIN
🐦   TWITTER
f    FACEBOOK

OBJECTIVE
To use my experience as a performer, entrepreneur, and marketer in my new career in live theater production. I hope to break away from my image as a puppet for the Disney Company and make a name for myself as a gritty, high-stakes Broadway producer.

PROFILE
The world's favorite mouse. Official mascot for the Walt Disney Company, with 88 years of experience in the entertainment industry. After several decades of working tirelessly to maintain my image as a cultural icon, I'm ready to move on and use my skills to save the struggling live theater industry.

PROFESSIONAL EXPERIENCE

**Video Game Work** 1987–Present
*Disney Interactive Studios*, Burbank, CA
Notable work includes *Epic Mickey* (2010) for Wii, *Disney's Magical Quest* (1992) for Super Nintendo, and *Mickey Mousecapade* (1987) for Nintendo.

**Theme Park Work** 1955–Present
*Walt Disney Parks and Resorts Worldwide, Inc.*, Various Locations
Work in several different roles at theme parks across the world, including those in France, Hong Kong, California, and Florida.
Head several park attractions.
Visit and take pictures with guests .

**Television Appearances** 1955–Present
*The Walt Disney Company*, Burbank, CA
Starred in *The Mickey Mouse Club* (1955–59. 1989–1996), a variety show featuring aspiring child and teenage artists.
Hosted and starred in *Mickey Mouse Works* (1999–2000) and *House of Mouse* (2001–2003).
Currently starring in *Mickey Mouse Clubhouse* (2006–Present) and *Mickey Mouse* (2013–Present).

**Feature Film Work** 1940–Present
*The Walt Disney Company*, Burbank, CA
Feature film career began with *Fantasia* (1940).
Other notable films: *Mickey's Christmas Carol* (1983), *Who Framed Roger Rabbit?* (1988), and *The Prince and the Pauper* (1990).

**Merchandising and Marketing** 1930–Present
*The Walt Disney Company*, Burbank, CA
Use likeness to promote Disney products and services worldwide through various media campaigns, including online, print, and film endeavors.
Serve as Official Disney Mascot.

**Comic Book Work** 1930–Present
*IDW Publishing*, San Diego, CA
Starred in several incarnations of Mickey Mouse comic books produced by various publishers over the years, including Dell Comics, Gold Key Comics, Gladstone Publishing, Gemstone Publishing, and Boom Kids!
Currently starring in the monthly comic, *Mickey Mouse*.

**Short Films** 1928–1952

*The Walt Disney Company*, Burbank, CA

Regularly starred in short films following 1928 debut in *Steamboat Willie*.

Still appears in shorts periodically, but now focusing mainly on longer form media and merchandising.

## EDUCATION

**Master of Fine Arts**                                        April 1961

California Institute of Arts, Valencia, CA

**Animation Course Specialization**                  June 1917

Chicago Academy of Fine Arts, Chicago, IL.

## ACHIEVEMENTS

| | |
|---|---|
| Academy Award for Best Animated Short Film, *Lend a Paw* | 1941 |
| Awarded star on Hollywood Walk of Fame | 1978 |
| Grand Marshal of the Tournament of Roses Parade | 2005 |
| Language competencies: Fluent in over 34 languages | |
| Immortality | |

# 3 TIME TO START WRITING: EVERYTHING YOU NEED TO KNOW ABOUT THE 8 RESUME SECTIONS (AND HOW TO WRITE THEM)

## Introduction

Let's be real: you're not reading this book because you think that resume writing is such a thrilling topic that you must devote hours of study to it. You're reading about this tedious topic because writing a resume is *difficult*. Well, all writing is difficult. But resume writing is even more challenging, because it's not exactly a choice. Sure, novelists may complain about writer's block, but that's the road they've chosen for themselves. (Hear that, novelists? Zip it!) This is not the case with the job seeker, who just wants to find fulfilling work.

The key to winning this battle is to tailor your resume for every job to which you apply. Yes, I said it—the key to successful resume writing is *more* resume writing. The way you write your resume depends on the position to which you are applying and the specific information that the hiring manager is looking for. As with any type of writing, defining the audience for your work makes producing that work quite a lot easier.

These are the eight sections of resume information that you will most likely need to include in your resume, at least to some degree:

✓ Contact Information

✓ Objective Statements

✓ Skills and Languages

✓ Education

✓ Employment

✓ Volunteer Experience

✓ Awards and Achievements

✓ References

## Section 1: Contact Information

Contact information is a resume must-have. Writing a great resume and forgetting to include your contact information is like going on an amazing first date only to realize afterward that you forgot to get the person's phone number or last name. While you're likely to work very hard to track that amazing person down, a potential employer is probably not going to do the same thing for you if you forget to include your contact information.

Here are the main things to keep in mind about contact information:

☆ Contact information should be listed first in the body of your resume

☆ Your name, address, phone number, and email should be included

☆ You can include a link to your LinkedIn profile, a fax number, or a cell number if you wish, but limit the amount of information you include in your contact information to avoid unnecessary clutter

Contact information is typically the first thing listed on your resume. Include your full name, address, phone number, and email. It may look something like this:

Most hiring managers tend to contact potential candidates by phone (as this is a chance to ask the individual a few preliminary questions), though some do use email to invite individuals to an interview. Make sure that you check your email regularly, though—it would be a shame to forget to check your email for a few weeks only to find out that you missed a date for an interview. If employers have difficulty getting in touch with you, they will move on to another candidate.

While contact information is fairly basic, there are some important points to consider:

- Provide a form of your name that you would use in your professional or personal life, but don't use a nickname

- Include an area code with your phone number

- Use an email that you will have access to on a consistent basis; for example, do not use a university email address that will expire when you leave the institution

- You may include a link to an online profile (such as LinkedIn), a fax number, or a cell number, but you should be selective in the amount of information provided so that your resume does not look cluttered or messy

What about including links to your other social media profiles in your contact information, such as Facebook, Twitter, or Instagram? This really depends on the specific field and the job to which you are applying. In creative or marketing-related fields, it may be appropriate to link to social media profiles. However, you *must* make sure that you are not only active on these social media profiles but also that the content is *professional* and *relevant to the position to which you are applying.* For example, let's say that you are applying to a marketing position and that you have built a substantial following on one of your social media profiles because you are an excellent artist. In this case, yes, including a link to the relevant social media platform is definitely important, as it demonstrates your ability to market your brand to a wide audience.

**Section 2:** Objective Statement

An objective statement is a brief, clearly written phrase that clarifies your career goals. It is traditionally included at the beginning of a resume. Sounds simple, but the question of whether to include an objective statement is anything but.

Some experts say that including an objective statement is a sure-fire way to make your resume appear outdated. Others argue that objective statements are essential because they give employers context to evaluate resumes and single out candidates whose goals meet those of the organization.

Let's get some perspective on this. While we can't provide a response that ends this conflict entirely, we can discuss some pros and cons to using an objective statement and suggest how to write an objective statement effectively, should you choose to use one.

Here are the basics of objective statements, and what will be covered in this section:

☆ Use an objective statement if you are just beginning your career and do not have enough experience to write an executive profile or career summary

☆ Make sure your objective statement is clear, focused, and relevant to the target position. Clearly link your career goals to those of the organization

☆ Most important, ensure that your objective statement identifies what you can do for the organization

## Pros and cons of objective statements

Here are a few reasons why an objective statement can be a good thing:

- ✓ It gives the employer an idea of how your career has been progressing and where you hope to go

- ✓ It lets you clarify what you want in your career

- ✓ It can help you ensure that your resume and career goals match the position

Here are a couple of reasons why an objective statement may be a bad thing:

- ✗ In the early stages of the recruiting process, the hiring manager likely has no interest in what *you* want

- ✗ These statements often come across as focusing entirely on the job seeker's personal objectives *rather than on the needs of the employer*

## Objective statements vs. executive profiles

Rather than using an objective statement, many career advisors suggest using executive or performance profiles, skills summaries, or career highlights. An executive profile, which summarizes the main qualifications you can bring to a job, may be a more effective way of identifying the most impressive aspects of your career, because it emphasizes what you can bring to the employer, rather than what the employer can do for you.

Still not quite getting the difference between an objective statement and an executive profile? Here's an example to help clear things up.

**Objective statement:**

> OBJECTIVE
>
> To use my experience as a performer, entrepreneur, and marketer in my new career in live theater production. I hope to break away from my image as a puppet for the Disney Company and make a name for myself as a gritty, high-stakes Broadway producer.

**Executive profile:**

> PROFILE
>
> The world's favorite mouse. Official mascot for the Walt Disney Company, with 88 years of experience in the entertainment industry. After several decades of working tirelessly to maintain my image as a cultural icon, I'm ready to move on and use my skills to save the struggling live theater industry.

The objective statement highlights some of the individual's strongest qualities, but it also focuses a bit more on what the position can do for the job seeker. In contrast, the executive profile focuses on what the potential candidate can do for the employer. The employer can pinpoint the value this individual would be able to bring to the company. Furthermore, the executive profile in the above example defines the candidate's experience.

### _How to create an effective objective statement_

Should you use an objective statement? If you are a seasoned employee, you should consider using an executive summary rather than an objective statement. However, if you are a job seeker who is just beginning your career, you may not have enough work experience to create an executive summary or career profile.

Here is a good formula to keep in mind when writing an objective statement:

**Target Position** (_experienced customer service representative_) +

**Linking Words** (_seeking to use my_) +

**Qualifications** (_client service skills_) +

**Potential Benefits to the Employer** (_to help improve customer relations_) =

_Experienced customer service representative seeking to use my client service skills to help improve customer relations._

These are features of a **good objective statement**:

✓ Brief and clear

✓ Relevant to the target position

✓ Specific (but not too specific)

✓ Links your career goals with those of the organization

✓ Sets you apart from other potential candidates by showing that you are a well-suited candidate

These are features of a **poor objective statement**:

✗ Vague and general

✗ Lacks focus

✗ Too specific (e.g., it only relates to one position offered at one company)

✗ Excessively wordy or convoluted

✗ Does not show employers that you have the skills they need

So...

**Don't** write this:

Seeking a position that will enhance my professional, customer service, and organizational skills.

**Do** write this:

Experienced customer service representative looking to use my client service skills to help improve customer relations.

And instead of this:

Looking for part- or full-time employment to help me pay off some of my debt.

**Do** write this:

Dedicated, experienced tutor seeking an opportunity to design user-centered activities to enhance student learning outcomes.

In a typical resume, place the objective statement after the contact information:

**BARBARA** MILLICENT **ROBERTS**

33 Continental Blvd • El Segundo, CA • 90245-5012
(+1) 310-252-3687 • workinggirl@therealbarbie.com

**OBJECTIVE** To gain employment with a respected university as a professor of medicine. My ultimate goal is to share my knowledge and experience with medical students aspiring to become skilled clinicians.

## Section 3: Skills and Languages

Skills sections are not typically included in traditional chronological resumes. However, this section is essential in functional and combination resumes. If you are using a chronological resume format and have specific skills that you would like to highlight (such as skills with specific programming languages), you might choose to identify these beneath the specific job (or program of study) in which you acquired these skills. You could also mention these skills in your objective statement or executive profile.

If you are using a functional or combination resume, a skills section can be a great way to highlight some of your most useful and relevant skills. Here are the main points to keep in mind when writing a skills section:

☆ Focus on occupational skills that are measurable and tangible

☆ Include only skills that can be measured and demonstrated (e.g., computer language proficiencies, typing speed, etc.); personal qualities (e.g., *hardworking, team player, organized*) should not be listed in the skills section

☆ Include the skills that are the most relevant to the target position

☆ If you are using a combination resume, include a profile of skills before your employment or education information

☆ If you are using a functional resume format, your skills section will make up the bulk of your resume, with three to five main categories of skills

☆ Include any languages in which you have written or verbal fluency. This may be a simple bullet point included in this section, or you may choose to include this information as its own subcategory within your skills section. If you do not have any languages that you wish to highlight in your resume, you can simply retain the title "Skills" for this section

## Who should include a skills section

Think of the field (or specific position) to which you are applying. The skills that you are outlining should clearly show the employer that you are qualified—the last thing employers want is to have to make the connection for themselves. In fact, an employer's greatest pet peeve is reviewing a resume that does not seem to fit the requirements of the position at all.

The skills section is usually presented after the contact information and objective statement. It includes the most useful, practical qualities of the applicant as they relate to the target position. As mentioned, this section is not typically found in chronological resumes, but it is key to functional and combination resumes. Certain types of employees will benefit most from a well-developed skills section:

- Those who have limited paid work experience in their field

- Those who have held many similar positions (making it redundant to list job duties under each job title)

- Those looking to make a transition into another field

### Combination resume formatting

If you are using a combination resume format, you will include a profile of skills, under which you provide a chronological listing of your employment history. Here are two formatted examples:

Option 1:

**Skills**
- Microsoft Suite (Word, PowerPoint, Excel, Outlook)
- Typing speed of 80 words per minute
- Programming languages (JavaScript, HTML, C#, Python)
- Mac and PC operating systems
- Basic accounting

Option 2:

**Skills**

Microsoft Office Suite    Programming languages        Bookkeeping

Mac and PC operating systems    Typing speed: 80 words/minute

Basic Accounting

### Functional resume formatting
If you are using a functional resume format, your entire resume will essentially consist of three to five sections that describe different categories of skills. Make sure that the subheadings you choose are broad enough that the general public would be able to understand them; avoid headings that may be too specific to your field.

Here is an example of the skills section of a functional resume:

Skills and Languages
- Microsoft Suite (Word, PowerPoint, Excel, Outlook)
- Typing speed of 60 words per minute
- Accounting/bookkeeping
- Fluently bilingual (English/French)

Professional Experience
**Customer Service**
- Greeted clients in a friendly and professional manner
- Used active listening techniques to address client concerns
- Maintained a professional demeanor during all interactions

**Office Work and Administration**
- Scheduled appointments for clients and rebooked when required
- Responded to in-person client inquires, as well as those made by phone or email
- Ensured that office equipment remained in proper working condition

**Computer Competencies**
- Designed company websites using JavaScript based on the principles of user-centred design
- Kept track of client files using Microsoft Excel, updating information as necessary
- Troubleshot computers to identify prominent system issues

## Section 4: Education

You worked long and hard for your education; make sure you use it to your greatest advantage. Many professions require that candidates have certain degrees, certificates, or diplomas from accredited academic institutions. Even if the specific position to which you are applying does not require that you have a certain educational background, the degrees you have obtained demonstrate your ability to meet strict deadlines, manage your time effectively, and achieve a difficult goal.

There's a lot to learn about the education section of your resume, but here are the key takeaways that will be discussed in the following section:

☆ Place the education section of your resume either after your employment history or following your objective statement/executive profile or profile of skills (depending on the type of resume); if the details of your education are more relevant to the position, then include this section first to ensure that it is prominent and noticeable.

☆ Provide information about your degree. The details of your education should be written in reverse chronological order and should include the official name of your degree, diploma, or certificate, as well as the academic institution, applicable enrollment dates, and major area of study (if applicable). If you have more than one degree, list them in reverse chronological order.

☆ List additional information (grade point average, scholarships, coursework, etc.) *if this information is relevant and meaningful to the position.*

## *What to include and how to format your education section*

You may be tempted to include many details of your education on your resume, but you should only include information relevant to the position to which you are applying. Here are more specific guidelines about which details should be provided and how to format them:

- **Degree name** — The degree name can be written in full (e.g., Bachelor of Arts in English) or abbreviated (B.A. in English), as long as you are consistent

- **School name** — The correct, official name of the academic institution must be included in full

- **Date of graduation** — Include the anticipated date (month and year) of graduation if you have not yet graduated

- **Grade point average (GPA)** — Include your GPA only if you believe it is high enough to give you an advantage over other candidates (i.e., it should be rather high)

- **Course names** — Only include course names and dates of completion if you are applying to a position that requires completion of certain academic courses. These should be listed below the official name of the degree or diploma in a bulleted list.

---

**Education**

**M.A. in English Literature and Creative Writing**                    2013–2015
*University of Windsor, Windsor, Ontario*

**B.A. in English Literature and Creative Writing**                    2009–2013
*University of Windsor, Windsor, Ontario*
- Relevant Coursework: Editing Practicum (2012); Publishing Practicum (2013)

---

You should focus on your post-secondary education, though you may include details related to your secondary education if you are currently enrolled in high school, or if the position to which you are applying requires a high school diploma. In addition to degrees or diplomas, you may also include

- Certificates or licenses (First Aid, CPR, etc.)

- Courses

- Training

- Any activities related to professional development that are pertinent to the position

If applicable, you may want to include a separate "Certificates and Licenses" section of your resume that is distinct from your educational history.

Where should you include your educational information when writing your resume? This depends on the job description. If you are applying to a job that does not require specific academic credentials, you may want to place the education section at the very end of your resume (following your professional work history). If the position clearly indicates that a degree is essential for the job, then your education should feature prominently on your resume so that employers can easily identify whether you have the necessary credentials.

**Section 5:** Employment History

Employment history is the first thing most people think of when writing a resume, and for good reason. Your employment history is the backbone of your resume. Without this support, your resume cannot stand on its own.

The exact formatting and placement of your employment history will vary depending on the type of resume you use. For more information on this, please see the next chapter.

Considering how important employment history is, there's a lot to learn about this aspect of your resume. Here's a breakdown of the main takeaways you should gain from this section:

- ☆ Provide your official job title, the name of the company, and the dates of employment. The number of positions you include may depend on how relevant your past experience is to the current position

- ☆ List your job duties beneath each job title, and make sure that these descriptive phrases are consistent in their grammar and sentence structure. Use the active voice, not the passive voice, to describe your duties and accomplishments

- ☆ Avoid including salary information, your reasons for leaving past positions, or false employment information

*Company and job title information*

The work experience section of your resume can be called "Work Experience," "Employment History," or simply "Experience." You may have many different types of experience that fall under this category, including:

- Part-time, full-time, or casual positions

- Fixed-term or ongoing employment

- Permanent or temporary positions

- Agency work

- Self-employment (e.g., freelance or contract work)

Whatever type the position may be, include:

- Your official job title

- Name of the organization

- Dates of employment

How far back should this chronological listing go? What about, for example, those nostalgia-inspiring years as a summer camp counselor back in college? Many career advisors suggest that you stick to the past 10 to 15 years, as the skills you gained beyond this range, though valuable, may be outdated. Sticking to a chronological listing of your employment over the last 10 to 15 years will also help you manage the length of your resume.

However, the 10-to-15 year rule is not appropriate for all situations. You might consider including experience beyond the past 10 to 15 years if:

- You are applying to a position that specifies 20 to 30 years of experience

- You are certain that your work history outside of the 10–15 year range is absolutely relevant to the position

You may also include the locations of the various organizations for which you have worked. The main thing is to be consistent.

| PROFESSIONAL EXPERIENCE | |
| --- | --- |
| **Video Game Work** | 1987–Present |
| *Disney Interactive Studios*, Burbank, CA | |

Please see "The Dos and Don'ts of Resume Organization and Design" for more information on the formatting of this information.

### Job duties and descriptions

List your primary job duties in a bulleted list beneath each job posting. These points should be written using the proper resume lingo described earlier in this guide. Use keywords and descriptors directly from the job posting to establish a clear link between your employment history and the position to which you are applying. These descriptors can be incorporated into the skills section of your resume if you are using a combination or functional resume, or you may include these descriptors when providing the details of your job duties. This means that you will probably have to edit and revise your resume (however slightly) for every position to which you apply.

Here are some examples of how job posting descriptors (underlined) can be incorporated into the job descriptions in your resume.

**Job posting:**

Intermediate knowledge of Microsoft Word and Excel

**In your resume:**

Drafted internal reports and documents using Microsoft Word and Excel

Let's look at one more:

**Job posting:**

Perform data entry and maintain client files

**In your resume:**

Updated client files regularly in an electronic database using data entry skills

The example below shows a portion of the employment section of a resume that has been tailored to a specific job posting.

**Job description:**

**Job title**: Medical Office Assistant
**Job type**: Part time
**Education**: Diploma in office administration
**Salary**: $20/hr
**Job Duties**:
- Greet patients and validate their health coverage upon arrival
- Schedule appointments
- Manage patient referrals
- Process internal documentation using an electronic file management system

**Required Experience**:
- One to two years of experience with office work and administration
- Excellent customer service skills
- Ability to work independently and as part of a team

In the example below, the action verbs are in bold and the quantified elements are in italics. Please note that this applicant has written about this position in the past tense, as the applicant is no longer employed by the Dental Health Centre in London, Ontario.

**Example employment section of a resume:**

*Receptionist & Accounts Assistant*
Dental Health Centre, London, Ontario
2010–2015
- **Informed** clients of their health care coverage
- **Scheduled** appointments for patients
- **Managed** up to *100 referrals per day*
- **Developed** an electronic management system that *reduced operating costs by 10% over 6 months.*

For each bullet point:

- Begin with a strong action verb that captures your primary job duties

- Aim for three to five bullet points beneath each element of your employment history

- Make sure that you consistently use the same tense within these bullet points; if you are currently employed at a position, use the present tense, but if you are no longer employed in the specific position, use the past tense

- Define your experience when applicable (performance metrics, percentages, time frames, etc.) to demonstrate your knowledge and skills

You may be tempted to use phrases like "Responsible for. . ." when describing your primary job duties. Three words: Don't do it. Passive descriptions have no place in resumes. Show, don't tell, the employer that you are skilled.

**Don't say this:**

Communicated effectively with all members of the team

**Do say this:**

Informed coworkers of monthly updates and revisions to document retention policies to ensure consistent practices among staff members

The first portion of this example does not prove to the employer that the candidate is able to communicate effectively. The corrected statement *shows* the employer how the potential candidate is able to use his/her communication skills in a way that is measureable.

*What not to include*
Although there is a lot of information to include in your employment

history, some information should be avoided at all costs. Luckily, the rules about what *not* to include are pretty clear.

Do not include:

- **Salary information.** Never include your past salaries. Salary information about the present position can be discussed at the interview if required.

- **Reasons for leaving past positions.** This information should also be excluded; you want your resume to leave a positive first impression on the employer. Any reasons for leaving past positions can be discussed at the interview stage.

- **False employment information.** You should *never* lie about your work experience. Even if your lies hold up long enough for you to acquire the position, you are unlikely to keep the job if your employer realizes that you exaggerated your abilities.

What if you don't have a lot of paid experience? You want to make your employment history seem substantial, but don't use sneaky tricks (like increasing font sizes or margins or using filler) to provide this substance. Employers have an eye for these kinds of tricks and do not look favorably upon them. The key to dealing with limited work experience is understanding that you have valuable skills; you just need to identify what they are. If you closely examine your informal work history (contract or project work, freelance positions, internships, etc.), you'll probably find that you have more experience than you thought. The example below shows the resume of an individual with limited work experience who has nevertheless held valuable year-long contract positions:

EDUCATION
**Honors Business Administration**
*University of Western Ontario, London, Ontario* 2004–2008
- Graduated with distinction

PROFESSIONAL EXPERIENCE
**Reference Assistant**
*Riverview Community Health Centre, London, Ontario* 2008–2009
- Provided reference assistance to students under the supervision of the head librarian
- Responded accurately and efficiently to student research inquiries
- Answered reference questions from students through email

**Student Marketing Intern**
*Winston Advertising, London, Ontario* 2007–2008
- Designed brochures and press releases with Photoshop, Adobe Illustrator, and InDesign
- Managed social media profiles (including Facebook and Twitter) to engage public interest
- Created marketing campaigns to help the company meet its strategic goal

Many employers will be wary of a candidate with clear gaps in employment. If you have significant gaps in your employment history, you should probably choose to use a functional or combination resume format, but there are other ways to deal with this (without lying or stretching the truth, of course).

- While it is necessary to include the dates for your past employment, omitting the months (while still including the years) can help disguise these gaps.

- You could also focus on what you did during the time when you were not employed. This may include volunteer experience, extracurricular activities, or community involvement (e.g., participating with committees on a voluntary basis). More on this is provided in the next section.

You should also understand that work experience does not necessarily need to be *paid* experience. Consider this from the employer's perspective; what does an employer really want to know? First, that you made valuable contributions to the organizations you worked for; and second, that you're able to transfer the skills you've acquired. This is true whether you were paid for the experience or not.

**Section 6:** Volunteer Experience

This section is an (unfortunately) overlooked and underappreciated step in completing a resume. Many experts in resume writing view volunteer experience as an optional section of your resume, but don't overlook the value of your volunteer experience. Including volunteer experience in your resume shows employers that you are willing to take initiative and get involved with your community—without expecting financial compensation.

There are a few key things to know about including volunteer experience on your resume:

☆ Include any voluntary positions you have held on a regular basis, as well as those you held for a limited amount of time (such as an unpaid internship)

☆ Choose whether to integrate your volunteer experience with your formal work history or include a distinct section titled "Volunteer Experience" or "Community Involvement" or something similar

☆ If you create a distinct section, format it to be consistent with that of your employment history

The volunteer positions you have held should include the same information you provide with your work experience:

- Job title

- Name of the organization

- Dates of employment

- Location

Again, try to be consistent. Beneath each voluntary position that you have held, include bullet points that describe the nature of your job duties, your major accomplishments, and your transferable skills.

VOLUNTEERING
**Chair**                                                                July 1885–Present
*Little Criminals Organization (LCO)*, London, UK
- Organize events to encourage children to pursue careers in the criminal arts
- Run workshops to teach basic crime skills, including lock picking, and psychological manipulation

**Dog Walker**                                                     January 1877–Present
*Royal Society for the Prevention of Cruelty to Animals*, London, UK

## **Section 7:** Awards and Achievements

You may choose to include a section outlining your awards and honors to help you stand out from other candidates. These achievements or awards do not necessarily have to apply directly to the job, but they should certainly demonstrate your ability to achieve excellence. This is an optional section.

This section may include:

☆ The official name of an award and/or achievement and the applicable dates (in reverse chronological order)

☆ Specific academic achievements (e.g., a high grade in a difficult course, an award, scholarships, academic honors)

☆ Professional awards, achievements, or honors (e.g., recognition for excellence by a professional organization)

Your awards and achievements section may look something like this:

| ACHIEVEMENTS | |
| --- | --- |
| Academy Award for Best Animated Short Film, *Lend a Paw* | 1941 |
| Awarded star on Hollywood Walk of Fame | 1978 |
| Grand Marshal of the Tournament of Roses Parade | 2005 |
| Language competencies: Fluent in over 34 languages | |
| Immortality | |

If you don't want to devote an entire section to awards and achievements, you may include these details in the skills section. You may also consider removing this section entirely if you only have one award or achievement that you wish to include here—you can simply provide this information with your education or professional history, as appropriate.

## Section 8: References

Some people claim that failure to include at least three references with every application gives employers a bad impression. Others note that it is presumptuous to provide references unless you are contacted for an interview. Who is right?

Here is what you need to know about including a reference section on your resume:

☆ Provide references *only when the employer specifically requests them*; this may be at the time of application, or it may be after an interview. If the employer is truly interested in hiring you, he or she will request references from you.

☆ *Do not* say "References available upon request." This *wastes the limited space you have to impress employers*. Employers know that you will be able to provide them with references if required.

☆ Try to use professional references. If necessary, you may also consider using coworkers or colleagues as references.

☆ Have a list of references prepared that includes the contact information of each individual. Always ask permission before using someone as a reference.

## Who to use as a reference

Many job postings require the names and contact information of at least three references. You should carefully consider the individuals you use as references on your resume. Potential references may include:

- Former employers or supervisors (from either paid or voluntary positions)

- Coworkers from current or past positions

- Colleagues (individuals who work in the same profession as you but not necessarily for the same company)

- Academic references, such as university professors or thesis supervisors

## Final checklist

Here is a checklist of everything you need in terms of your resume sections. Double check to make sure you've included:

- Your address, phone number, email, and relevant social media links in your contact section

- An objective statement or career summary that is relevant to the position and identifies the skills you can bring to the job

- A list of skills and languages that provides a clear link between

your professional qualifications and the job requirements (if you are

using a functional or combination resume format)

- A section that outlines your post-secondary education, including the names of all degrees/diplomas/certificates, enrollment dates, and relevant coursework, as well as any licenses or additional certifications

- Your employment history, including your job titles, the names of the organizations for which you have worked, dates of employment, and descriptions of your job duties

- Your volunteer experience

- A section that outlines any awards or professional achievements you may have

- And, finally, if requested in the job posting, the names, titles, and contact information for each of your references

Now that we've covered the eight sections of a resume, let's take a closer look at how to design and organize your resume.

# 4 THE DOS AND DON'TS OF RESUME ORGANIZATION AND DESIGN

## Introduction

Pretend for a moment that you are the busy hiring manager for a credit union. You are in the process of reviewing hundreds of resumes for a job opening within the company. You have very limited time to spare. You come across a resume that includes large blocks of text, inconsistent formatting, and various fonts. Let's say it looks something like the sample below:

# Jane Smith

1234 Main St • Windsor, Ontario • (123) 555-5555 • my.name@email.com

**OBJECTIVE**
Experienced customer service representative looking to use my client service skills to help improve customer relations.

SKILLS AND LANGUAGES
- Microsoft Office (Word, Excel, PowerPoint, Outlook)
- Active listening techniques
- Excellent verbal and written communication skills
- Typing speed of 60 words per minute
- Fluently bilingual (English and French)

**EDUCATION**
Bachelor of Arts in English Literature
McGill University, Montreal, Quebec                    2008–2012

- Graduated with distinction

- $4000.00 entrance scholarship

**EMPLOYMENT**
*Full-time Service Representative*
Royal Bank of Canada, Windsor, Ontario                2013–Present
- Promote current and upcoming services to clients
- Understand and find solutions to client concerns
- Recruit potential clients by understanding their financial needs

Customer Experience Representative, 2009–2012
Chapters, Montreal, Quebec
- Assisted customers with finding desired materials
- Greeted all customers and assessed their needs
- Replenished stock and processed store products

*Cashier*                                             2005–2007
Shopper's Drug Mart, Windsor, Ontario
- Maintained checkout and customer service areas
- Processed customer orders
- Interacted with customers in a friendly, professional manner

**VOLUNTEER EXPERIENCE**
*Youth Tutor*, 2005–2006
New Canadians' Center for Excellence, Windsor, Ontario
- Instructed students in basic English writing and reading skills
- Engaged students using active learning techniques

1234 Main St • Anytown, State/Province, Country • Postal/Zip Code • (123) 555-5555 • my.name@email.com

The inconsistent formatting makes this resume difficult to read and interpret. What is the likelihood that an employer will take the time to sift through this information to see if the candidate is ideal for the position? Remember, employers spend very little time reviewing resumes. They may be inclined to toss your resume aside if they are immediately affronted by a text-heavy document plagued by inconsistent formatting.

Without the use of proper resume formatting, it won't matter how impressive your credentials are. You must use proper formatting if you're going to grab a potential employer's attention quickly. With this in mind, here are the most important things to consider when formatting your resume:

- ✓ Font usage

- ✓ Headings and formatting

- ✓ White space

- ✓ Customization

- ✓ ATS accommodation

## Choosing the Right Font

The font you use in your resume has a direct impact on readability. Just imagine how a busy hiring manager would deal with a resume that is actually *difficult* to read. Never overlook the importance of choosing the right font. There are a few main points to keep in mind when it comes to font selection:

- ☆ Select fonts that are legible and professional

- ☆ Make sure that the type of font you use is consistent throughout your resume

- ☆ Ensure that the font is large enough to be readable but not so large that it makes your resume unnecessarily long

## Serif or Sans-Serif

Fonts come in two main categories: serif and sans-serif. Serif fonts have added flourishes at the ends of letters, while sans-serif fonts do not. Some example fonts are listed below:

Serif Fonts

- Times New Roman
- Garamond
- Courier
- Cambria

Sans-Serif Fonts

- Arial
- Helvetica
- Calibri
- Century Gothic

It is perfectly acceptable to use two fonts within your resume. For example, you may want to use a serif font for the headings of your resume and a sans-serif typeface for the main text. Avoid the temptation to use flowery or fancy fonts. No matter how nice you think a fancy font may look, the use of a non-standard font does not look professional, and these fonts are often difficult to read.

Bold and italicized fonts are great options to help certain elements of your resume stand out (such as section headings or job titles), but do make sure that these font treatments are applied consistently throughout your resume.

Select a font size that is readable (you don't want readers to have to strain their eyes to read your resume), but you also want to make sure that the font is not too large, because this will make your resume unnecessarily long.

### Headings and Formatting

We have already discussed the various types of headings that are commonly used in resumes to distinguish an applicant's employment history, education, and contact information. Be sure to format these headings neatly and consistently to keep your resume readable and professional. The other information in your resume, like the details of your employment history and academic experience, must also be formatted consistently. Here are the main things to keep in mind:

- ☆ Format headings so that they are easily distinguishable from the main text

- ☆ Keep your headings and other formatting consistent

The hiring manager reviewing your resume should be able to distinguish the headings from the main text quickly and easily. To keep the headings distinct from the body of the resume, use one or a combination of the following:

- Include a single line space before or after a main heading.

- Make the headings bold.

- Use a larger font size for the headings.

- Center the headings while keeping the rest of the text left justified.

In addition to formatting your headings, you must also decide how to format the information in the main body of your resume. You have many options to choose from; just make sure that your resume remains legible and appealing.

Let's look at employment history in a chronological resume as an example. When formatting the details of your employment history, add:

- The name of the company

- Dates of employment. Right-justified employment dates are most common because they are the easiest to find

- Your title

### Using White Space

Another essential element of designing a modern, professional resume is white space. *White space* is exactly what it sounds like: blank space with no text or images. Incorporating white space in a resume can be difficult. After all, you have a lot of information to include! However, using white space will help your resume appear more balanced, and it will also help the individual reviewing your resume easily identify the most important elements of your professional history.

Here are the main points to keep in mind to make sure your resume has enough white space:

- ☆ Use simple, direct language; remove articles and personal pronouns where applicable. This reduces the number of words, thereby increasing the amount of white space.

- ☆ Avoid using full paragraphs or long sentences.

- ☆ Use the "quadrant test" to determine whether the text in your resume is evenly distributed.

How you write your job descriptions can influence the amount of white space in your resume. Remember when we discussed how to describe job duties in a resume? Personal pronouns and other nonessential words are often removed. Not only does this leave you with short and powerful statements, but it also reduces the total amount of text you'll need to include in your resume. Complete sentences or full paragraphs, on the other hand, take up unnecessary space.

How can you be sure your resume has the balance it needs and properly uses white space? You can quickly check this using something called the "quadrant test." Just print off a draft of your resume and divide it into four sections, then measure whether the text is evenly distributed in each section.

*Custom formatting and resume templates*

Some resume writers use multiple colors and unique design elements to highlight specific aspects of their resumes. This can be appropriate if you're applying to certain positions (graphic designer, for instance). But if your resume is intended for a conservative company (say, an accounting firm), it's best to avoid colors and fancy designs.

Let's talk a bit about ready-made resume templates. A simple online search will provide thousands of free resume templates. Resume templates consist of fields and tables in which you can simply insert the necessary information. The benefit of using these templates is that they make formatting a resume simple and straightforward. However, make sure that you make the necessary changes to ensure that the document does your unique history and professional background justice. A resume template may use a chronological format, but if you feel that a combination format is best for you, be sure to add a skills section.

### *Variations in length*

The length required for a resume depends entirely on the individual's unique background. Generally speaking, a resume—not to be confused with a *curriculum vitae*, which can be much longer—should be one or two pages long.

You should consider limiting your resume to one page if:

- You are a recent graduate with no extensive work experience

- You are using a functional resume format to highlight specific skills

- You would have a hard time filling two complete pages with relevant information

Consider a two-page resume if:

- You have extensive education and/or work experience that is relevant to the position to which you are applying

- You are applying for a senior or executive position

- You are applying for a complex position that requires the use of many different skills

The important thing to keep in mind when it comes to resume length is this: Your resume should be no longer or shorter than it needs to be to tell prospective employers everything they need to know.

*Including a photo in your resume*

You may think that using a photo is a great way to customize your resume and make it stand out. However, if you are applying for jobs in North America or the United Kingdom, including a photo of yourself in your resume would be a mistake. The aversion to using photos in resumes is particularly pronounced in the United States and the United Kingdom. Here are some of the pros and cons of using a picture on your resume:

**Pros:**

- Including a photo in a resume may be beneficial for certain professions (namely acting and modeling)

- We live in an age in which social media dominates, and many applicants have LinkedIn profiles with their picture (which hiring managers often look at when evaluating applicants)

**Cons:**

- Using a picture in your resume will not inspire a hiring manager to examine your resume longer or more carefully than those of other applicants

- Legally, hiring managers must remain objective when evaluating resumes. A photograph gives the hiring manager clues about specific personal details, such as an applicant's race, gender, age, etc.

- Including a photo in a resume may (unfortunately) increase your chances of being discriminated against

Whether you agree with the use of photos in resumes or not, as a job applicant, you should be aware that there is a general dislike of this practice.

### Formatting with an ATS in mind

In your efforts to beat ATSs, you must pay close attention to formatting.

**Do**

- ✓ Stick to simple formatting

- ✓ Include the contact information in the body of your resume

- ✓ Use simple fonts, such as Arial, Impact, Georgia, or Courier

- ✓ Ensure that your resume is free of spelling errors

- ✓ Save your resume as a basic .doc or .txt file

**Don't**

- ✗ Include images, columns, text boxes, or complex graphics

- ✗ Place your contact information in the header (don't use a header at all)

- ✗ Use underlining, bolding, or italics

- ✗ Use special characters or fancy bullets

- ✗ Use excessively flowery or specialized fonts

Some design features may help your resume look professional and distinguished when you are submitting a hardcopy, but complex designs can make it very difficult for an ATS to process your resume. The use of tables, columns, figures, images, graphics, and text boxes make it especially difficult for an ATS to read the data contained within these design features.

We previously noted that bolding or italicizing text is a great way to ensure that the elements of your resume are easily distinguished from one another (e.g., headings versus job titles). However, these features are not recommended for use with ATSs. Therefore, make sure that you have an ATS-friendly version of your resume that uses simple formatting. It is perfectly acceptable to use bold and italicized font when submitting your resume as a hardcopy, but do have a version that is suited to ATSs at the ready.

Special or nonstandard font types easily confuse ATSs. Try to stick to conservative business fonts, such as Arial, Times, Impact, or Courier. Special font treatments (e.g., underlining text) can sometimes make it difficult for an ATS to read lowercase letters like y, j, or g, so avoid underlining text if possible. Be aware that ATSs can have difficulty reading specific characters or accents on letters (for example, an é may render as a question mark).

Another element to consider is the use of bullets. ATSs do not usually have issues with bullets. However, ATSs are sometimes unable to decipher checkmarks or other special bullet types.

Finally, be aware of the file format in which you save your resume, because some ATSs may be unable to process the information in unique file types. The safest file formats are .doc or .txt files (rather than .pdf, .rtf, or .jpg).

# 5 THE THREE DEADLIEST RESUME ERRORS (AND HOW TO AVOID THEM)

You've certainly come a long way in your resume writing journey. You've learned what to include in a resume, how to write each section, and how to tailor your resume for each job you seek. Now that you know what you *should* do, it's time to review what you absolutely, under no circumstances *ever*, should NOT do when writing your resume.

You may recall some of the errors brought up in earlier chapters. Here's a quick recap of the advice for avoiding errors that has already been discussed at length.

- Avoid generic, meaningless buzzwords, such as *results-oriented*, *team player*, *hardworking*, *detail-oriented*, etc.

- Do not make claims about your abilities. Instead, describe accomplishments that *demonstrate* your abilities

- Avoid wordiness. Use short, straightforward sentences. Remove personal pronouns and small words like *a, an, or,* and *the*

- If you use an objective statement, make sure it clearly states how your skills will contribute to the company's success

- Do not use a generic resume for every position; rather, tailor your resume to each specific position

In addition to the errors we've discussed at length, there are also some embarrassing and horrific mistakes that can completely destroy your job prospects to avoid making when writing your resume. These errors can completely zap the credibility of the most carefully crafted resume.

✓ *Do not* leave grammar or spelling errors in your resume

✓ *Do not* include irrelevant information (e.g., personal details about your non-work-related interests)

✓ *Do not* lie or exaggerate to make yourself look better

Avoiding these errors may seem simple enough, but without the proper knowledge, making these common errors is easier than you may think. Let's look at each of them in greater detail.

## Spelling and Grammar Errors

We've mentioned a few times now that it doesn't take much for an employer to discard your resume forever. While you may not have an eye for grammar and punctuation, it's very possible that your potential employer does—in fact, nearly 60% of employers view grammatical or spelling errors within a resume as a primary reason for immediately disqualifying an applicant. Even one or two teeny, tiny spelling, grammar, or punctuation errors within your resume can land your resume in the discard pile.

So, what should you look for when proofreading your resume? Common errors include:

- Improper spelling and capitalization

- Incorrect punctuation usage, especially commas and semicolons

- Use of incorrect words, especially homonyms (e.g., *you're* versus *your*; *lose* versus *loose*)

- Subject–verb agreement errors

- Inconsistent verb tense (e.g., neglecting to use present tense when describing your current position and past tense when describing responsibilities at your past jobs)

- Errors in your contact information, such as incorrect email address or phone number

A resume with spelling or grammatical errors gives the employer a bad impression of the applicant. Unfortunately, it is difficult to catch punctuation or grammatical errors within a resume, even if you read it repeatedly. Here is a remedy: once you have edited the document, try to find another individual to read your resume. Having a friend or family member review your resume is one way to check for errors. Nothing is more effective than a fresh pair of eyes when it comes to editing. You may also consider checking out the writing and proofreading services available at the nearest career center, library, or university. A professional resume editing service, like the one offered by Scribendi.com, is a great choice if you are not confident in your writing skills.

### Irrelevant Information

Some types of information just don't belong in a resume, though applicants are often tempted to include them:

- Personal or demographic information, like age, marital status, and gender

- Personal identification numbers, like social insurance or social security numbers

- Information about hobbies or activities unrelated to the position

While you should never list irrelevant hobbies or activities on your resume, it *is* a great idea to mention hobbies and activities that closely relate to the job duties required of the specific position.

For example, your work fundraising for your local humane society may be relevant for a prospective position as a veterinary assistant. Your avid interest in taxidermy, however, is less likely to catch the hiring manager's eye.

Remember that you should never share personal or identifying information with anyone other than your actual employer.

### Lying or Exaggerating

This resume mistake is important. Of all the information provided in this book, please take this to heart: never lie, exaggerate, or otherwise stretch the truth on a resume.

There are many ways that you might stretch the truth on your resume. For example, you might:

- Fluff the details of your education

- Exaggerate the role you played in a certain work position

- Make up a position you never held for a company you never worked for

Telling a little white lie on a resume might seem like a harmless way to increase your chances of finding employment. Though some cases of resume falsification may be unintentional, it is easy for a small exaggeration to become a very serious problem down the line. Even something that seems like a small lie can come back to haunt you. Let's say, for example, that you claim to have a master's degree from an esteemed institution, but though you did *attend* the institution, you never actually graduated from it. A white lie of this type may not seem like a terrible idea, but what happens when you are asked to prove your claims are true?

## The potential consequences of lying on your resume

Even if lying gets you to the interview stage, many employers will perform a background check to verify your credentials. However, some employers extend a job offer prior to discovering that a candidate has potentially falsified his or her credentials.

*If employers discover that someone they've hired has lied about his or her academic or professional history, the employer will very likely terminate the employee immediately.* This means that all the hard work you put into your resume will have gone to waste, and your professional reputation will also take a serious hit.

Resumes that Win

# Morgan Le Fay

1234 Main St • Windsor, Ontario, Canada • Y74 I9U
**CELL** (123) 555-5555 • **EMAIL** morganlefay@email.com

| | |
|---|---|
| SUMMARY | Qualified professional with more than five years of experience as a dental hygienist and with strong interpersonal communication skills. |

| | | |
|---|---|---|
| ACHIEVEMENTS | **Leadership Award, Canadian Dental Hygienist Association** | 2014 |
| | Recognition for Excellence in Customer Service | 2007 |

| | | |
|---|---|---|
| EDUCATION | **Dental Hygiene Program** | |
| | St. Clair College, Windsor, Ontario | 2005–2008 |
| | Graduated with honours | |

| | | |
|---|---|---|
| EMPLOYMENT | **Dental Hygienist** | 2012–Present |
| | South Shore Dental, Kingsville, Ontario | |

- Evaluate patients' oral health, including their overall dental hygiene
- Design individualized dental healthcare plans in consultation with the dentist
- Perform general office duties, as required

| | |
|---|---|
| **Pediatric Dental Hygienist** | 2008–2012 |
| Dentalcorp, Thornhill, Ontario | |

- Cleaned patients' teeth and gums
- Applied topical fluoride treatments to repair tooth damage
- Organized patient health records in a web-based file management system

| | |
|---|---|
| **Part-time Cashier** | 2008–2012 |
| Zehrs, LaSalle, Ontario | |

- Scanned and processed customer purchases quickly and efficiently
- Ensured product knowledge remained thorough and up-to-date
- Maintained the appearance of the check-out area

| | | |
|---|---|---|
| VOLUNTEERING | **Internship** | |
| | Eastside Dental Office, Windsor, Ontario | 2010–2012 |

- Assisted the dental hygienist during dental check ups
- Organized patient records

Chronological resume

# THOMAS KIDD

1234 Main St • Montreal, Quebec, Canada • P9C F6U
(123) 555-5555 • kidd_t@email.com

**OBJECTIVE** Seeking a position as an art teacher in a secondary school setting in which I can use my knowledge of best practices in instruction to improve student learning outcomes.

**EDUCATION**

**Bachelor of Education**
McGill University
Montreal, Quebec
2003–2005

**Bachelor of Fine Arts**
University of Windsor
Windsor, Ontario
1999–2003

**SKILLS**
Learner-centred education
Designing learning objectives
Photography
Digital imaging
Sculpting
Painting (watercolor and oil)
Sketching and drawing

**PROFESSIONAL EXPERIENCE**

**Teaching and Education Skills**
- Prepared instructional material
- Tailored instruction according to learning goals and objectives
- Evaluated student progress and identified problem areas

**Artistic Knowledge and Skills**
- Developed artistic content across physical and digital platforms
- Encouraged students to use cutting-edge techniques to create unique designs and projects
- Worked with Adobe Photoshop and Adobe Illustrator

**EMPLOYMENT HISTORY**
Supply Teacher, 2005–2012
Assistant Art Class Instructor, 2003–2004
Part-time Tutor, 2001
Cashier, 1998–1999

Functional resume

# MONICA GELLER

Suite #202, 10th Street • Manhattan, New York • (226) 858-5555 • themonicageller@email.com

EXECUTIVE PROFILE

Experienced culinary professional with extensive knowledge of safe food handling, culinary practices, and kitchen management. Thorough knowledge of safety and health regulations.

SKILLS

Hospitality Services
Kitchen Management
Baking and Pastry
Nutrition
Food Safety
Current Safe-Food Handling Certificate

EDUCATION

**Culinary Management Program**
George Brown College, Toronto, Ontario                           2010–2012

EMPLOYMENT

**Executive Chef**                                                2015–Present
*Oakwood Resort, Manhattan, New York*

- Oversee a culinary team of sous chefs and prep cooks
- Manage food costs
- Ensure that all staff members consistently adhere to food safety guidelines and practices

**Cook**                                                          2010–2014
*Seasons Retirement, Manhattan, New York*

- Prepared meals for residents according to their dietary needs and restrictions
- Ordered food and other kitchen supplies, as needed
- Operated food production equipment

**Prep/Line Cook**                                                2008–2010
*Crabby Joe's, New York, New York*

- Communicated with other kitchen staff members to ensure that all orders were of the highest quality and were delivered to customers on time
- Assembled consistently high-quality meals for customers
- Processed incoming orders

VOLUNTEERING

**Community Garden Volunteer**
*Ward Acres Community Garden, New Rochelle, New York*

Combination resume

# 6 THE BEST IS YET TO COME: FINAL REMARKS

Congratulations! You now know everything there is to know about how to create the very best resume to fit your specific needs. As you've surely learned by now, resume writing is much more than drafting a simple document that outlines your work history. Your resume must reflect not only the experiences and accomplishments you've already achieved, but also what you are *capable* of achieving. If your resume doesn't "sell" you as an employee, it's not doing its job, and you'll never *get* your job. No pressure, right?

It's true that social media profiles like LinkedIn and Google+, as well as online job application systems, are having an effect on how we seek employment. Though these tools are central to networking and job searching, resumes remain the main vehicle through which individuals communicate their qualifications to potential employers. And in this fast-paced world where employers are said to spend less than ten seconds reviewing a resume, your resume needs to stand out. Just like any other form of writing, crafting the perfect resume is about hooking your potential employer by appealing to their interests and needs. Considering the employer's perspective is paramount to writing the ideal resume, a point which we hope has been made clear throughout this guide.

If we have succeeded in our mission, you now know how to accurately convey your own personal brand, highlight your most significant professional accomplishments, and capture the interest of the hiring manager or employer. In short, you have all the skills and knowledge you need to land that new and exciting position you've been waiting for.

We hope this guide to resume writing has served *you* just as well as your new resume will serve your future employer. Now that you know how to tackle the sometimes grueling task that is resume writing, you can start looking forward to achieving your ultimate goal—getting the job you want and deserve. And really, what could be more exciting than the prospect of a new career path?

And now, dear reader, it is time for you to spread your job-seeking wings, finish your resume, and get yourself out there. *But wait,* you may be thinking, *what if I'm not ready?* Putting yourself out there can be fairly intimidating. Ask yourself this: are you hesitating because you're nervous, or because you feel like there's still more to learn about creating the perfect resume? If you've used this guide to craft a well-tailored resume, it's time to put your skills to the test and start applying for jobs. However, if you're still feeling overwhelmed by the sheer amount of resume-writing information in this book, why not check out Inklyo's companion course, *Resume Writing that Works: How to Write the Perfect Resume*? This course helps break down the information found in this book and provides a step-by-step guide to resume creation. When it comes to something as important as your career, it never hurts to be extra thorough!

## *Works Consulted*

Adams, Susan. 2012. "What Your Resume Is Up Against." *Forbes*. Last modified March 26, 2012. http://www.forbes.com/sites/susanadams/2012/03/26/what-your-resume-is-up-against/.

Adams, Susan. 2014. "The Best and Worst Words to Use on Your Resume." *Forbes*. Last modified March 17, 2014. http://www.forbes.com/sites/susanadams/2014/03/17/the-best-and-worst-words-to-use-on-your-resume/#176f552c33e4.

Aquino, Judith. 2011. "HR Execs Reveal the 13 Most Common Resume Blunders." *Business Insider*. Last modified May 19, 2011. http://www.businessinsider.com/worst-resume-blunders-2011-5?op=1.

Asghar, Rob. 2013. "'No Photo on Your Resume' and Other Career Advice You Should Question." *Forbes*. Last modified July 22, 2013. http://www.forbes.com/sites/robasghar/2013/07/22/no-photo-on-your-resume-and-other-career-advice-you-should-question/#3c19d4cc4ab7.

Beal, Peter. 2008. "Résumé." In *Dictionary of English Manuscript Terminology 1450–2000*, edited by Peter Beal. Oxford, UK: Oxford University Press. Available online. http://www.oxfordreference.com/view/10.1093/acref/9780199576128.001.0001/acref-9780199576128.

Birkel, Damian. 2013. *The Job Search Checklist*. USA: AMACOM. Online edition. http://proquest.safaribooksonline.com.proxy3.library.mcgill.ca/book/career-development/9780814432914/step-4-crafting-an-effective-r-sum/chap10_xhtml?uicode=mcgill.

Board of Regents of the University of Wisconsin System. 2014. "The Writer's Handbook: Resume Writing Tips." *The Writing Center at the University of Wisconsin-Madison*. Last modified August 27, 2014.

https://writing.wisc.edu/Handbook/Resume.html#breadth.

Boston College Career Center. 2015. "How to Write a Resume." *Boston College*. Last modified August 18, 2015. http://www.bc.edu/offices/careers/jobs/resumes/howto.html.

Burns, Karen. 2010. "The Most Powerful Words to Use on a Resume." *US News & World Report: Money*. Last modified November 24, 2010. http://money.usnews.com/money/blogs/outside-voices-careers/2010/11/24/the-most-powerful-words-to-use-on-your-resume.

CareerBuilder, LLC. 2011. "Your Work History: How Far Back Should You Go on a Resume?" *CareerBuilder*. Last modified August 3, 2011. http://advice.careerbuilder.com/posts/your-work-history-how-far-back-should-you-go-on-a-resume.

CareerBuilder. 2013. "CareerBuilder Releases Study of Common and Not-so-Common Mistakes that Can Cost You the Job." *CareerBuilder.* Last modified September 11, 2013. http://www.careerbuilder.com/share/aboutus/pressreleasesdetail.aspx?sd=9%2f11%2f2013&siteid=cbpr&sc_cmp1=cb_pr780_&id=pr780&ed=12%2f31%2f2013.

CBS News. 2010. "Terms to Never Use in Your Resume." *CBS News*. Last modified April 24, 2010. http://www.cbsnews.com/news/terms-to-never-use-in-your-resume.

Dooley, Eileen. 2012. "Reference Etiquette: Boost Your Resume with Strong Contacts." *The Globe and Mail*. Last modified September 6, 2012. http://www.theglobeandmail.com/report-on-business/careers/career-advice/reference-etiquette-boost-your-resume-with-strong-contacts/article533691/.

Dummies.com. "The Essentials of Preparing a Resume." *For Dummies, a Wiley Brand*. Accessed October 26, 2015. http://www.dummies.com/how-to/content/the-essentials-of-preparing-a-resume.html.

Eastern Illinois University. "Chronological Resume vs. Functional
    Resume: What's the Difference?" *Eastern Illinois University*.
    Accessed October 28, 2015.
    http://www.eiu.edu/careers/chrono_functional_resumes.php.

Environment Canada. 2013. "Resume Tips." *Government of Canada*. Last
    modified July 9, 2013. https://www.ec.gc.ca/emplois-
    jobs/default.asp?lang=En&n=031AD043-1.

Green, Alison. 2011. "Ignore these 10 Outdated Pieces of Career
    Advice." *US News & World Report*. Last modified July 11, 2011.
    http://money.usnews.com/money/blogs/outside-voices-
    careers/2011/07/11/ignore-these-10-outdated-pieces-of-
    career-advice.

Half, Robert. 2014. "10 Things Not to Include When Writing a Resume."
    *CareerBuilder*. Last modified August 29, 2014.
    http://advice.careerbuilder.com/posts/10-things-not-to-
    include-when-writing-a-resume.

Huhman, Heather. 2012. "Which Resume Type is Right for You? The
    Pros and Cons of Three of the Most Popular Resume Formats."
    *US News & World Report: Money*. Last modified February 3,
    2012. http://money.usnews.com/money/blogs/outside-voices-
    careers/2012/02/03/which-type-of-resume-is-right-for-you.

Issacs, Kim. "How to Use Resume Samples Effectively." *Monster*.
    Accessed March 12, 2016. http://career-
    advice.monster.ca/resumes-cover-letters/resume-writing-
    tips/how-to-use-resume-samples-effectively-
    canada/article.aspx.

Issacs, Kim. "Is a Combination Resume Right for You?" *Monster.*
    Accessed April 6, 2016. http://www.monster.com/career-
    advice/article/is-a-combination-resume-right-for-you.

Jouliot, Erin. 2015. "How to Integrate Volunteer Experience into Your
    Resume." *University of Connecticut Center for Career
    Development*. Last modified March 5, 2015.

http://career.uconn.edu/blog/2015/03/05/how-to-integrate-volunteer-experience-into-your-resume/.

Joyce, Susan P. 2014. "Customize Your Resume in 5 Quick Steps." *Huffpost Business.* Last modified July 19, 2014. http://www.huffingtonpost.com/susan-p-joyce/customize-your-resume_b_5343814.html.

Jyoti, Christine Ryan. 2014. "9 Resume Mistakes You Can't Afford to Make." *Forbes Personal Finance.* Last modified April 2, 2014. http://www.forbes.com/sites/learnvest/2014/04/04/resume-mistakes-you-cant-afford-to-make/#16eea1025e97.

Kennedy, Joyce Lain. 2011. *Resumes for Dummies.* Hoboken, NJ: Wiley Publishing, Inc. Kindle edition. http://www.amazon.ca/Resumes-Dummies-Joyce-Lain-Kennedy/dp/0470873612.

Ladimeji, Kazim. 2014. "Is It Finally Okay to Include a Photo in Your Resume?" *Recruiter.* Last modified August 7, 2014. https://www.recruiter.com/i/is-it-finally-okay-to-include-a-photo-in-your-resume/.

Learn How to Become. 2015. "The Importance of Volunteer Work." *Learn How to Become.* Accessed March 28, 2016. http://www.learnhowtobecome.org/volunteer-and-nonprofit-careers/.

Learning Express Library. "Great Resumes: Experience." *Learning Express Library.* Accessed November 16, 2015. http://www.learningexpresshub.com/productengine/index.html#/startCourse/48d74a60-b7fa-4899-a51f-4c5e6a51aa38/learningexpresslibrary.

Levin-Epstein, Amy. 2012. "How far back should your resume go?" *CBS News Money Watch.* Accessed April 8, 2016. http://www.cbsnews.com/news/how-far-back-should-your-resume-go/.

Lublin, Daniel A. 2006. "Lying on Resumes." *Metro*. Accessed March 28, 2016. http://www.toronto-employmentlawyer.com/lying-on-resume-gets-you-fired/.

Ma, Wenlei. 2014. "Should You Include a Photo with Your Resume?" *News.com.au*. Last modified May 29, 2014. http://www.news.com.au/finance/work/should-you-include-a-photo-with-your-resume/story-fnkgbb6w-1226935711818.

Macfadyen, Sarah. "The Ultimate Resume Checklist." *Inklyo.com*. Accessed February 27, 2016. https://www.inklyo.com/ultimate-resume-checklist/.

Manning, Kelsey. 2014. "What Social Media Accounts Should You Include on Your Resume?" *Levo.* Accessed April 6, 2016. http://www.levo.com/articles/career-advice/what-social-media-accounts-should-you-include-on-your-resume.

McCarthy, Amanda, and Kate Southam. 2014. *Writing Resumes and Cover Letters for Dummies*. Australia: Wiley Publishing Australia Pty Ltd.

Mesan, Char. 2014. *Right Your Resume: Fix or Create Your Resume Content so You Can Stand out and Impress the Hiring Manager*. Penrith, Australia: Char Mesan Enterprises. Available online. https://goo.gl/4wqehc.

Messer, Max. 1999. "Avoiding the Cardinal Sins of Resume Writing." In *Job Hunting for Dummies, 2nd Ed.* Foster City, CA: IDG Books Worldwide. Available online. http://www.dummies.com/how-to/content/avoiding-the-cardinal-sins-of-resume-writing.html.

Michigan State University. "Action Verbs." *Michigan State University: Career Services Network*. Accessed October 28, 2015. http://careernetwork.msu.edu/resources-tools/resumes/action-verbs.html.

Monster.com. "Functional Resume Sample." *Monster*. Accessed February 26, 2016. http://career-advice.monster.com/resumes-cover-letters/resume-samples/sample-of-a-functional-resume/article.aspx.

Morrow, Valerie. 2014. "How Do I Handle Employment Gaps on My Resume?" *Grantham University Blog*. Last modified February 14, 2014. http://blog.grantham.edu/online-degree-program-employment-gap-tips.

Nisen, Max. 2013. "Moneyball at Work: They've Discovered What Really Makes a Great Employee." *Business Insider*. Last modified May 6, 2013. http://www.businessinsider.com/big-data-in-the-workplace-2013-5.

Olson, Angie, Allen Brizee, and Katy Schmaling. 2013. "When to Use Two Pages or More." *Owl Purdue Online Writing Lab.* Last modified March 12, 2013. https://owl.english.purdue.edu/owl/resource/571/1/.

Olson, Lindsay. 2012. "5 Essential Tips When Using a Resume Template." *US News & World Report: Money.* April 19, 2012. http://money.usnews.com/money/blogs/outside-voices-careers/2012/04/19/5-essential-tips-when-using-a-resume-template.

OWL Purdue. "Work Experience Section." *OWL: Purdue Online Writing Lab*. Accessed November 17, 2015. https://owl.english.purdue.edu/owl/resource/565/03/.

Purdy, Charles. 2015. "Ten Words and Terms that Ruin a Resume." *Monster*. Accessed October 27, 2015. http://career-advice.monster.com/resumes-cover-letters/resume-writing-tips/10-words-ruin-resume/article.aspx.

Resume Genius. "Resume Format Guide – Reverse-Chronological, Functional, and Combination Styles." *Resume Genius*. Accessed February 12, 2016. https://resumegenius.com/resume-formats.

"Resume Writing Checklist." *Stetson University Career Services.* Accessed April 9, 2016.

http://www.stetson.edu/administration/career-and-professional-development/media/pdfs/resume_checklist.pdf.

Rose, Angela. "Easy Steps to Customize Your Resume for the Job You're Applying for Right Now." *Hcareers.* Accessed January 23, 2016. http://www.hcareers.com/us/resourcecenter/tabid/306/articleid/1027/default.aspx.

Rosenberg, Arthur D. 2008. *The Resume Handbook Fifth Edition: How to Write Outstanding Resumes & Cover Letters for Every Situation.* Avon, Massachusetts: Adams Media, 2008.

Scribendi.com. "A Combination Resume Example." *Scribendi.com.* Accessed February 27, 2016. https://www.scribendi.com/advice/combination_resume_example.en.html.

Scribendi.com. "Combination Resumes! Targeted Resumes! Mini Resumes! Which Do I Choose?" *Scribendi.com.* Accessed November 3, 2015. http://www.scribendi.com/advice/combination_resumes_and_targeted_resumes.en.html.

Service Canada. "Job Search Safety Tips." *Job Bank: Service Canada.* Accessed January 30, 2016. http://www.jobbank.gc.ca/content_pieces-eng.do?cid=5003.

Service Canada. 2011. "Resumes: Awards/Achievements." *Job Bank: Service Canada.* Last modified November 30, 2011. https://www.jobsetc.gc.ca/eng/pieces.jsp?category_id=222&root_id=201.

Services for Youth. 2015. "Writing a Resume." *Government of Canada.* Last modified May 22, 2015. http://www.youth.gc.ca/eng/topics/jobs/resume.shtml.

Skillings, Pamela. 2012. "The New Grad's Map to Resume Writing." *Big Interview*. Last modified June 28, 2012. http://biginterview.com/blog/2012/06/resume-writing-new-grads.html.

Stein, Marky. 2009. *Fearless Resumes: The Proven Method for Getting a Good Job Fast*. New York, NY: McGraw Hill.

Sundberg, Jörgen. "Don't Use a Resume Template if You Want to Land a New Job." *Undercover Recruiter.* Accessed March 12, 2016. http://theundercoverrecruiter.com/dont-use-resume-template-if-want-land-new-job/.

Tonge, Lee. 2013. "CV Design Using the Quadrant Method." *The CV Store.* Last modified August 15, 2013. http://www.thecvstore.net/blog/cv-design-quadrant/.

United States Probation and Pretrial Services: Western District of Washington. "Resume, Cover Letter & References." *US Probation and Pretrial Services: Western District of Washington.* Accessed January 21, 2016. http://www.wawp.uscourts.gov/resume-cover-letter-references.

University of Wisconsin. "Resume Guide: Layout and Design." *University of Wisconsin – Eau Claire Career Services.* Accessed January 23, 2016. http://www.uweccareerservices.org/resume_guide/design/index.html.

University of Toronto Mississauga. "First-Time Resume Writing." *University of Toronto Mississauga.* Accessed December 28, 2015. https://www.utm.utoronto.ca/careers/first-time-resume-writing.

University of Wisconsin-Madison. 2014. "The Writer's Handbook: Resume Writing Tips." *The Writing Center at the University of Wisconsin-Madison.* Last modified August 27, 2014. https://writing.wisc.edu/Handbook/Resume.html#sections.

Vaas, Lisa. "Resume Objective Statements to Catch a Manager's Eye." *The Ladders.* Accessed November 10, 2015. http://www.theladders.com/career-advice/resume-objective-statements-catch-managers-eyes.

Vault.com. "Resume Samples: Chronological Resumes." *Vault*. Accessed February 26, 2016. http://www.vault.com/resumes/sample/chronological-resumes/marketing-entry-level-chronological-resume-summary-lead.

Virginia Technic Institute and State University. 2013. "References: Guidelines for Your Job Search." *Virginia Tech: Division of Student Affairs.* Last modified November 12, 2013. http://www.career.vt.edu/JobSearchGuide/ReferenceGuide.html#when.

Virginia Technic Institute and State University. 2015. "Contents and Sections of Your Resume." *Virginia Tech: Division of Student Affairs*. Last modified October 7, 2015. http://www.career.vt.edu/resumeguide/ContentSections.html.

Walker, Rob. 2015. "The Performance Art of Resumes." *The New York Times.* Last modified May 2, 2015. http://www.nytimes.com/2015/05/03/jobs/the-performance-art-of-resumes.html

Whitcomb, Susan Britton. 2010. *Resume Magic: Trade Secrets of a Professional Resume Writer, 4th Ed.* Indianapolis, IN: JIST Works. Available online. https://www.safaribooksonline.com/library/view/resume-magic/9781593577339/.

White, Martha C. 2013. "5 Things You Should Absolutely Never Put on a Resume." *Time.* Last modified November 11, 2013. http://business.time.com/2013/11/11/5-things-you-should-absolutely-never-put-on-a-resume/.

Yate, Martin. 2012. *Knock 'Em Dead Resumes: How to Write a Killer Resume that Gets You Job Interviews, 10th ed.* Avon, Massachusetts: Adams Media. Available online. http://www.amazon.com/dp/1440536813/ref=rdr_ext_tmb.

Yate, Martin. 2014. *Knock 'Em Dead 2014: The Ultimate Job Search Guide.* Avon, Massachusetts: Adams Media. Available online.

http://windsor.lib.overdrive.com/0D82D09B-DF35-41F2-91B8-FF3487917881/10/50/en/ContentDetails.htm?id=868C5D54-AC2F-44C3-ADD4-6E845A0B8F8F.

## About the Author

Inklyo.com is the provider of a wide and ever-growing selection of resources to help anyone become a better writer. Offering online courses, ebooks, and articles, Inklyo.com delivers a high-quality writing education to people of all ages and skill levels, from English-language learners looking to understand the basics to writing pros looking to apply their skills in a new career.

Backed by more than 20 years of experience in the document revision industry, the members of the Inklyo.com team—who are writers and editors themselves—understand the importance of clear and accurate writing. This is reflected in the quality of Inklyo.com's resources, which have been the recipients of a Global Ebook Award, WebAward, and International Business Award.

Connect with Inklyo.com online:

**Twitter**: https://twitter.com/inklyo

**Facebook**: https://www.facebook.com/inklyo

**Google+**: https://plus.google.com/+Inklyo

**LinkedIn**: https://www.linkedin.com/company/inklyo

**Email**: https://www.inklyo.com/contact/

**Blog**: https://www.inklyo.com/blog/

If you liked this book, please visit https://www.inklyo.com/books-on-writing/ to download our other titles:

*How to Write an Essay in Five Easy Steps*

*Effective Business Communication*

*How to Write a Letter*

*How to Write a Blog*

*Unlocking the Art of Fiction Writing*

*The Complete Guide to the Parts of Speech*

*The Complete Guide to Sentence Structure*

Did you find this ebook helpful? If so, consider leaving us a review on the Amazon page of the book you enjoyed or over at GoodReads.com!

39308346R00057

Made in the USA
Middletown, DE
11 January 2017